PLEASURE TRIPS BY UNDERGROUND

Jonathan Riddell

Capital Transport

ACKNOWLEDGMENTS

First published 1998

ISBN 185414 200 3

Published by
Capital Transport Publishing
38 Long Elmes
Harrow Weald
Middlesex

Designed by Tim Demuth

Printed in Singapore
by CS Graphics

© London Transport Museum
and Capital Transport Publishing

The author would like to thank his colleagues at the London Transport Museum for their help in the production of this book, particularly David Ellis, Robert Excell, Helen MacKintosh, Hugh Robertson and Sheila Taylor.

NOTE ON POSTER SIZES

Most Underground posters appeared in one of three standard sizes. By far the most common was double royal (25ins by 40ins), which could be doubled to form quad royal (50in by 40in). Another common size was double crown (20in by 30ins). The small panels which appeared inside the vehicles were printed in a variety of sizes to fit the locations for which they were intended.

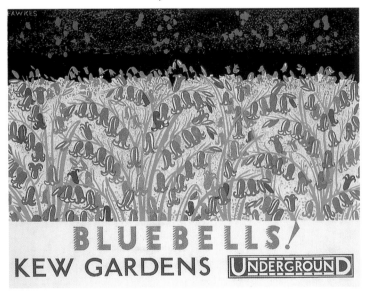

Bluebells!
Panel poster
IRENE FAWKES 1931

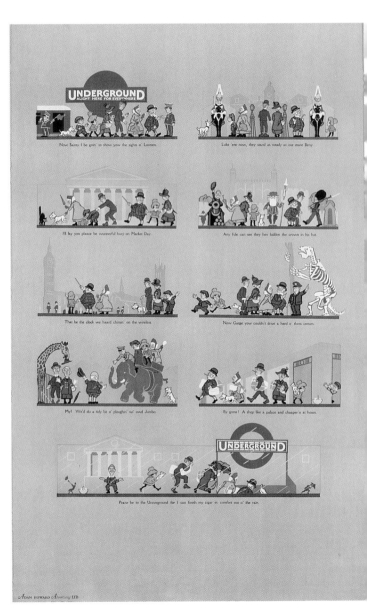

Alight Here for Everywhere
Double royal poster
ADAM HOWARD 1927

CONTENTS

From Country to the Heart of Town
Double royal poster
DORA M BATTY 1925

In and Around London
Leaflet 1932

INTRODUCTION

Cheap Return Tickets
Double royal poster
EDWARD McKNIGHT KAUFFER 1927

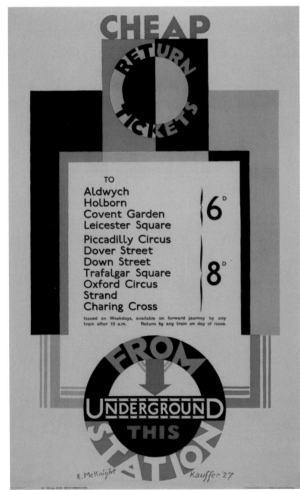

The Underground first opened in 1863 since when people have used it both for business and pleasure trips. Perhaps not surprisingly commuters have traditionally been considered the more important sector, simply because they have always represented the greatest number of passengers. For instance, by the mid-1930s sixty per cent of London Transport's passengers travelled during the rush hours of 7 am to 10 am and 4 pm to 7 pm on weekdays. With spare seats at other times, the Underground soon realised the opportunities presented by promoting leisure travel.

Looking around, they could see the main line railway companies hard at work promoting their services. The LNER used artists of the calibre of Tom Purvis to advertise its North Sea resorts. The GWR employed, amongst others, Edward McKnight Kauffer (an American artist originally discovered by the Underground). His posters and guide books encouraged passengers to sample the delights of Devon and Cornwall, while the LMS Railway commissioned the celebrated French artist Cassandre to design posters promoting the company itself rather than named destinations. Even the Southern, best known for its commuter services, produced a wide variety of attractive material enticing potential passengers to enjoy the hidden delights of Surrey (such as its lake district) and the exotic Isle of Wight. Continental travel was also advertised by those railways with connecting ferry services to the continent.

The Underground could not compete with the main line railways in the range of destinations and distances covered. But, with a wealth of major attractions within London and a countryside which still reached close into the centre of London, it was possible to advertise a surprisingly wide number of destinations and variety of attractions. These included palaces and museums, parks, countryside and even the sea. In 1908 the Underground began to publish its own stylish advertising material and by the 1920s was equalling, if not surpassing, its much larger rivals in the field of poster art in particular, and design in general.

The phenomenal success of the Underground's posters rested in the hands of one man, Frank Pick. A solicitor by training, Pick joined the Underground in 1906 and soon took control of its publicity, which at the time lagged behind the best that the other railways could offer. Pick realised that almost every type of attraction in London was within reach of the Underground, or at least could be marketed as such. He believed very strongly in the need to educate Londoners about the attractions on their own doorstep, and much of his publicity was based on this central concept. At the same time he understood the need to create a clear corporate image, with a distinctive look.

In the field of publicity Pick did not try to change posters, handbills and leaflets all at once, but concentrated at first on the posters. If one compares the Underground's posters between 1908 and 1920 with its publicity, it is obvious that the handbills and leaflets represent an earlier period stylistically. While Pick knew that he could not change everything at a stroke, the delay in updating the style of the leaflets was aggravated by the First World War. As a result, it was not until

Come Out! Easter by Train
Double royal poster
MAJOR 1931

the early 1920s that the great improvement could be seen in the design quality of the Underground's publicity leaflets.

Not all improvements came to a halt because of the war. Kauffer, who became one of England's foremost poster artists, was first commissioned by Pick during 1915. Another major innovation which appeared during the war was the Johnston typeface. Originally designed to be used for Underground station names, it was soon adapted to suit other purposes and by the 1920s began to appear on posters and other publicity. Surprisingly for a commissioned typeface and in a company with a strong feel for corporate design, the new typeface was not adopted universally. Artists often designed their own lettering as an integral part of the poster and even when they did not, the Johnston typeface was often passed over in preference for a style of lettering felt to be more suited to the subject.

Before the introduction of new publicity materials the early tube railways were not a financial success, and more passengers were needed. Already aware of the importance of encouraging off-peak leisure travel the Underground issued a variety of tickets for such use. In 1938 London Transport's Annual Report records the number of special tickets issued for use on its railways, trams and trolleybuses:

Cheap return tickets into and out of London ... 18,500,000
Cheap all-day tickets 30,500,000
Cheap mid-day tickets 49,000,000
Cheap evening tickets 26,500,000
Pleasure party tickets 500,000
Sports club tickets 500,000

With the exception of the Cheap mid-day tickets, which were generally only valid on the company's trams and trolleybuses, all these tickets could be used on the Underground trains. Again, Pick used posters and leaflets to advertise the availability of these types of tickets, with or without a suggested destination.

It must be remembered that until the formation of London Transport in 1933, although the Underground Group operated a large proportion of the capital's public transport network, it did not control all forms of public transport. The main exceptions to the Underground Group's operation were the Metropolitan Railway, which had a much more extensive system than today's Metropolitan Line, and the London County Council Tramways. Both these companies produced their own distinctive publicity. The LCC Tramways, in particular, produced an attractive series of posters in the 1920s and early 1930s.

Shop by Underground
Double royal poster
ALDO COSOMATI 1926

'*Shopping must be reckoned among the pleasures. Certainly so far as the principal shops and stores of the West End are concerned*' London Transport wrote in its Annual Report for 1938. By the time the first tube railways were being constructed in London the Victorian department store was already well established and London's importance as Britain's shopping capital was perhaps even greater than it is now. With the expansion of London westwards from the City, the main shopping areas within London migrated from the City to the West End, with stores such as Whiteley's opening its first shop in Westbourne Grove in 1863, to expand to ten shops by 1872. This rate of expansion may have been assisted by the construction of the sub-surface railways and, at the turn of the century, by the new tube railways, particularly the Central London Railway. The fortune of some areas, such as Bayswater, may have fluctuated. But for the period covered by this book, and even today, it is Oxford Street, Regent Street, Bond Street and Piccadilly, known as the West End, that can be seen as the centre for its variety of shops. Other areas were noted for particular types of goods or a specific department store. The geography of shopping is still changing, as it will probably always be doing. But, between the First and Second World Wars, out of town shopping centres, such as Brent Cross, did not exist. The effect they were to have may have been countered by the importance of the suburban high street which was, in many respects, greater than it is now.

With this in mind, the Underground's posters and other publicity material were primarily aimed at encouraging its passengers to travel to the West End where they could enjoy leisured and luxurious shopping, instead of a short walk to the local high street shops. The Underground usually did not promote any individual shop, however famous it might be. An exception was a small illustrated publicity leaflet, dating from 1910, which listed a number of shops by name.

Thus, the posters advertising shopping fall into two main categories: those promoting a particular shopping season such as Christmas shopping or the summer or winter sales, and those encouraging the shopper to travel outside the peak hours. Often both messages would overlap, with posters beckoning to the delights of the Christmas shops but also giving advice to travel between the hours of '10' and '4'.

Until the Second World War it would have been normal for the man to be the breadwinner and his wife to be looking after the home. So many, if not all, posters were targeted mainly at the housewife, who would have had the freedom to travel while the husband worked in the office. Normal office hours then included Saturday mornings, and afternoons as well were not unusual. To take advantage of this market segment the Central London Railway, which became part of the Underground Group in 1909, experimented with special season tickets for its women passengers – but only during January, the period of the winter sales.

Cheap Day Return Tickets
Double royal poster
CHARLES PEARS 1930

Apart from the press advertisement on page 11, this is the only other image of a shop interior. The woman shopper sitting relaxing on a stool while being served at the counter at once reinforced the message that shopping by Underground could be an enjoyable and pleasant pastime.

Shops and Stations
Press advertisement
C H JACKSON 1930

The Underground used advertisements in the newspapers to complement its poster campaigns. Of the stations listed, Dover Street is now named Green Park, Post Office is now St Paul's, Strand is now Charing Cross, Aldwych is now closed and Queens Road is now Queensway.

SHOPS AND STATIONS

The Shops	*The Stations*
BOND STREET	Bond Street
	Dover Street
BROMPTON ROAD	Knightsbridge
CHEAPSIDE	Post Office
HOLBORN	Holborn
	Chancery Lane
HIGH ST. KENSINGTON	High Street Kensington
KNIGHTSBRIDGE	Knightsbridge
OXFORD STREET	Oxford Circus
	Tottenham Court Rd.
	Bond Street
PICCADILLY	Piccadilly
REGENT STREET	Piccadilly
	Oxford Circus
STRAND	Strand
	Trafalgar Square
	Aldwych
TOTTENHAM COURT RD.	Tottenham Court Rd.
	Goodge Street
VICTORIA STREET	St. James Park
	Victoria
WESTBOURNE GROVE	Queens Road

Between 10 and 4—
Your best shopping hours. More comfort—greater speed—Cheap Shopping Tickets are issued daily after 10 a.m.

UNDERGROUND

E3/411/30

These two posters, issued three years apart, use exactly the same text and very similar images; women holding umbrellas against a winter storm. But with his different treatments Kauffer has been able to create two quite different posters. Over the years Kauffer's signature changed many times, reflecting the different influences on his work.

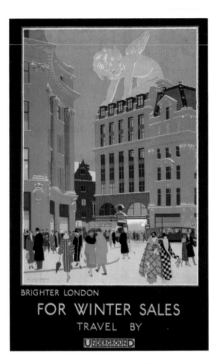

Brighter London for Winter Sales
Double royal poster
HAROLD SANDYS WILLIAMSON 1924

This is one of the few shopping posters to depict a seemingly realistic street scene, albeit with a rather large and presumably benevolent white figure over the building in the background. With London's main shopping streets so well known, the lack of realistic street views in the company's posters may have been because the Underground did not want to be seen promoting any one shop over its rivals.

Winter Sales *Double royal poster*
ANONYMOUS 1920

The clock face, with the hours of *10* and *4* highlighted, dominates not just the image but the entire theme of the poster.

The Way to Winter Sales
Double royal poster
REGINALD P GOSSOP 1927

Your Guide to Winter Sales
Double royal poster
REGINALD P GOSSOP 1928

Each year, from 1925 to 1928, the Underground produced colourful decorative poster maps in which the West End's main shopping streets – Oxford Street, Regent Street, Bond Street and Piccadilly – were highlighted. Similar maps were also produced by Gossop to encourage travel to the theatres.

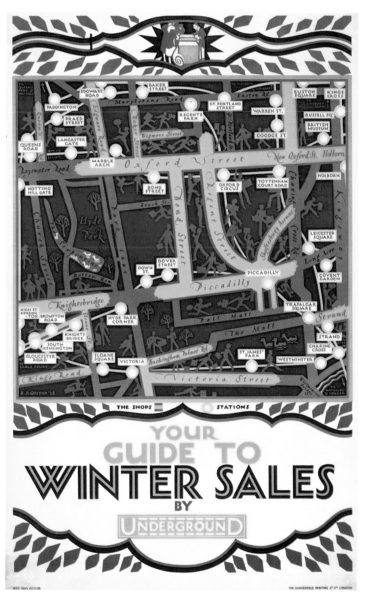

Shop between 10 and 4
Double royal poster
EDWARD MCKNIGHT KAUFFER 1930

Another interpretation using the clock face. This poster was one of two by Kauffer to encourage off-peak travel. The other was called *Play between 6 and 12*.

Christmas Shopping
Press advertisement
ANONYMOUS 1926

The advantage of advertising in the newspapers was that it could reach people, such as housewives, who did not regularly travel by tube. This would particularly apply at Christmas when people might wish to travel to the West End for the stores.

Shop between Ten and Four
Double royal poster
FLETCHER 1926

In this poster the clock face has been used to show the contrasting scenes of peak-time crush and off-peak calmness. In common with much of the Underground's publicity at the time, the passengers shown are elegant and middle class, suggesting that the Underground was a form of travel to be aspired to by the working classes.

Christmas Shopping
Press advertisement
C H JACKSON 1930

Jackson's drawing of men and women shoppers being served at a busy counter was also used in a panel poster. The Cheap Shopping tickets referred to in the advertisement are in fact ordinary cheap day return tickets.

It's Better to Return Early
Double royal poster
CLIFFORD and ROSEMARY ELLIS
1935

It's Better to Shop Early
Double royal poster
CLIFFORD and ROSEMARY ELLIS
1935

During December there was a need to encourage shoppers to spread the days on which they shopped, as well as to avoid the rush-hours.

Toyland, Mobilising for Christmas
Double royal poster
TONY SARG 1914

In 1913 the Underground issued a monthly series of 12 posters, called *Humours of London*, by the artist Tony Sarg. This is an adaptation of *In Toyland* which formed part of the series. The main image in the top half remains the same, but the text

Into the Heart *Quad royal poster*
ANONYMOUS 1909

The image of a typical wet and wintry street scene contrasts strongly with the view of a warm and brightly lit interior of an Underground train. The two images had also been used separately on double royal posters the previous year.

and characters in the lower half have been altered by replacing the family group with toy soldiers in modern khaki and horse-drawn guns and ambulances. When this poster was first issued for Christmas in 1914 the First World War had just started and this would have been seen as a popular and patriotic version of the usual Christmas poster.

To the Shopping Centres
Double royal poster
GLADYS MARY REES 1920

The striking image of Father Christmas on this poster makes the words almost superfluous. However, as the Underground also issued posters wishing passengers a Merry Christmas, copy was added to encourage them to travel by Underground to the shopping centres.

Christmas – Shop Early between 10 & 4 *Panel poster*
EDWARD McKNIGHT KAUFFER 1923

This poster combines the messages to shop early in the Christmas month and to shop between 10 and 4, but the name *Underground* does not appear. It was probably for posting inside Underground carriages.

Shop between 10 and 4
Double royal poster
GLADYS MARY REES 1920

In this poster the artist has used the image of an elegant and middle class mother with her two children (flanked by figures carrying the numbers '10' and '4') to illustrate the unhurried pleasures of mid-day shopping. At the bottom of the poster is the contrasting image of chaos caused by hurrying commuters (all men) during the morning and afternoon peaks. This poster also appeared as half of a quad royal poster; with the main shopping streets listed on the other half, making it the first 'pair poster' to appear on the Underground.

For Christmas Shop
between 10 & 4 *Double royal posters*

AUSTIN COOPER 1924
HORACE TAYLOR 1924

During the 1920s the Underground often issued two Christmas posters. Contrasting styles by Austin Cooper and Horace Taylor are shown here.

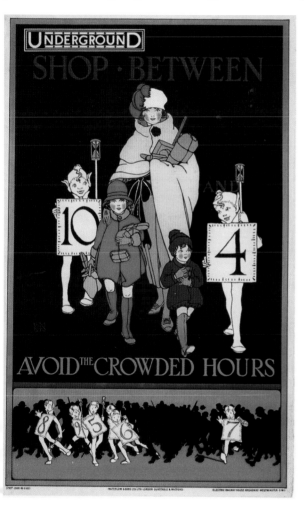

From Country to the Heart of Town
Double royal poster
DORA M BATTY 1925

The Underground realised that most shoppers would not, nor could not, use their railway services to travel from the country into the centre of London as its lines did not extend far enough and bus, coach and main line railways were already providing direct services. There are two other posters in this series promoting travel by Underground between the country and London, one advertising theatres and dances and the other, picnics and rambles.

Summer Sales Quickly Reached
Double royal poster
MARY KOOP 1925

This is the only poster by Mary Koop produced by the Underground, but it is similar in style and typographical treatment to a series of posters of similar vintage by Horace Taylor.

Do your Shopping Early
Panel poster
FOUGASSE (CYRIL KENNETH BIRD)
1936

This simple poster, with its giant figure of Father Christmas overpowering a small man, is typical of the artist's work. Fougasse is best known for his Second World War propaganda posters, particularly the series *Careless Talk Costs Lives*.

The Underground Puts the Shops on your Doorstep *Press advertisement*
ANONYMOUS 1925

This advert written in verse is clearly aimed at the middle class female market.

Please Shop Early
Panel poster
FOUGASSE (CYRIL KENNETH BIRD)
1937

Do your Shopping Early
Panel poster
FOUGASSE (CYRIL KENNETH BIRD)
1936

The poster with its mass of colourful flags looks like a patriotic celebration of the Coronation of King George VI. But it was issued for a more mundane purpose, namely to remind the public that it would be best to shop before Coronation day when several central London stations would be closed.

A NIGHT OUT

**BRIGHTEST LONDON
AND HOME BY
**

Brightest London and Home by Underground *Double royal poster*
HORACE TAYLOR 1924

While its bright and stylish image encourages people to enjoy an evening in the West End, the poster also reminds them that they can still travel home by Underground at the end of the evening.

In the 1920s and 1930s cinemas and theatres were highly popular. With their ability to attract huge audiences it is not surprising that the Underground was keen to promote them, particularly as their patronage increased travel in the quiet period after the early evening peak. In the 1930s there were 49 theatres in central London, similar to the number today, but serving a smaller population. As most travelled by Underground, the dispersal of theatre audiences in the West End actually created a minor traffic peak.

In addition to theatres and cinemas, there were many other types of entertainment to be found in the West End at night. Even the Zoo had late night opening during the summer months. Although London Transport collected statistics on the numbers who visited theatres and cinemas, it could not compile them for those who enjoyed dancing, cabaret or dining. Even so, it was obvious that people would visit London to enjoy all aspects of night life, so the Underground covered these themes in many memorable posters. There was, however, one exception which was never chosen as the subject of a pictorial poster; that was visiting the pub. This had to wait until the 1980s for a pictorial poster to be issued. Some sports fixtures, such as speedway and dog racing, were also held in the evening.

With the exception of one or two posters advertising the Proms, the Underground did not use its pictorial posters to advertise particular performances. Although leaflets, press advertisements and some general posters named some or most of the theatres, the Underground usually took good care not to show favouritism by highlighting one venue more than another. The commercial advertising of an individual play or film was left to the promoter or venue concerned.

Unlike some other metro systems, the Underground has never operated 24 hours a day and so could not provide a service to those wishing to stay in town after midnight. For the majority of visitors to the West End this was not a problem, as there was still plenty of time to catch the Tube home well after the entertainment had finished.

To the Restaurants
Double royal poster
MAURICE BECK 1933

London Transport occasionally produced photographic posters. The photographers employed were usually credited on the posters, and included well known names such as Man Ray. Because of the type of photo-lithographic process used to print them, the results often look dated compared with their hand-drawn counterparts.

Why go home? *Double royal poster*
MARC SEVERIN 1938

In 1938 London Transport ran a poster campaign to encourage Londoners to stay in town for an early evening meal after a day in the office, and thereby ease the rush hour.

Why home so soon?
Double royal poster
MARC SEVERIN 1938

Another poster in the series suggests that there is no need to rush home after an evening's entertainment, but instead stay and enjoy a meal in town.

The Circus *Double royal poster*
CHARLES ATKINSON 1933

Atkinson's poster of the Circus is
unusual, not in the choice of subject
or artistic style, but because it was
produced in two parts. The image
of the circus was printed separately
and designed to be placed over the
poster background carrying the
lettering.

Bertram Mills' Circus *Panel poster*
BRIAN ROBB 1937

Bertram Mills' Circus *Panel poster*
HERRY PERRY 1938

Along with pantomimes, circuses provided popular
Christmas family entertainment. The use of animals
performing would not be acceptable on today's posters.
If it were not for the bullseye on the box, Robb's poster
could be mistakenly thought to have been produced by
Bertram Mills instead of London Transport.

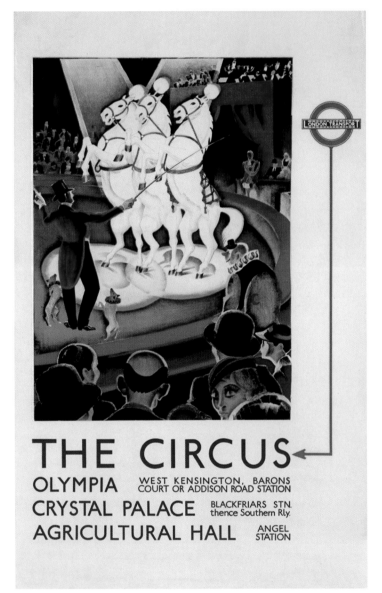

The Road to Pleasure *Panel poster*
Anonymous 1909

The diners in their Edwardian clothes look very dated when compared to Taylor's art deco poster of 1924 on page 16, but the Great War had intervened and society was very different.

Play between 6 and 12
Double royal poster
Edward McKnight Kauffer 1931

By following the latest artistic trends and adapting them for commercial design, Kauffer remained at the forefront of poster design. Over the years his style changed several times, and in the early 1930s he was strongly influenced by Modernism as shown by this poster.

Come out to Play *Panel poster*
Clifford and Rosemary Ellis 1936

London Transport could only benefit by encouraging season ticket holders to stay in town later and ease the homeward rush hours.

This poster was issued as part of a campaign to encourage more passengers to buy season tickets.

Hearing the Riches of London
Double royal poster
F C HERRICK 1927

Herrick, who for many years was the Head of Studio at the Baynard Press, produced 46 posters for the Underground. This poster formed part of a series depicting the five senses. Each poster included a modified bullseye worked into the design.

Late Theatre Trains *Leaflet*
ANONYMOUS 1909

According to the print code at the base of this leaflet, 250,000 were printed. The tube trains and tunnels border was used on a number of leaflets and was probably pre-printed in some millions – hence the code finding itself overprinting the border.

Many of the theatres shown on the map have now disappeared. Today, the Savoy is the only theatre left on the south side of the Strand. Ironically, when Aldwych station (then called Strand) opened in 1907, it displaced the Strand Theatre, only to have the Underground's late night theatre trains extended to start from there.

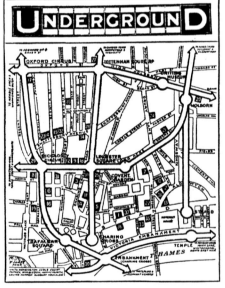

We're off to the Pantomime
Double royal poster
MABEL LUCIE ATTWELL 1913

Throughout the twentieth century pantomimes have been one of the most successful forms or theatrical entertainment. With the exception of this poster by the famous children's illustrator Mabel Lucie Attwell, the Underground issued few pantomime posters before the Second World War.

For Christmas Plays
Double royal poster
ALBERT RUTHERTSON 1923

This was the second Underground poster Ruthertson designed as a children's toy theatre. Other posters designed to be made into toys included a model railway, complete with track, trains and stations and a model bus. All these, like Underground posters generally, were available for purchase.

FOR CHRISTMAS PLAYS

The Theatres *Panel poster*
HERRY PERRY 1934

This unusually proportioned and conceived poster by Herry Perry comes from a set of four depicting: dining-out, sightseeing, visiting friends and the theatre, all set in period costume. On each poster, the half bullseye advertises a different aspect of London Transport's operations, namely: UNDERGROUND, TRAMWAYS, GREEN LINE, GENERAL, the last named still being used for buses at the time.

THE THEATRES

ALL SERVED BY UNDERGROUND

Design for Playgoers
Double royal poster
O'KEEFFE 1935

Two years after H C Beck's
diagrammatic Underground map
first appeared, O'Keeffe used the
concept as a basis for a series of
posters encouraging leisure travel
to London.

London's Offer *Double royal poster*
LEWITT-HIM (JAN LE WITT and
GEORGE HIM) 1938

The outstretched arms appearing
from behind the theatre curtain
hold in their hands representations
of some of the different pleasures
that could be enjoyed during a
night in town.

Variety and Review
Press advertisement
W A HARRISON 1934

Ballet by Underground
Double royal poster
STANISLAUS LONGLEY 1933

In this small poster words are not needed, the picture of three ballerinas (later used by Fitton) says all that is needed to convey the message.

Ballet – Just a Step by Underground *Quad royal poster*
JAMES FITTON 1937

Fitton's poster was printed in two halves to form a quad royal poster. After the Second World War, artists were often given a complete double royal poster in which to develop their designs, the other double royal sheet being overprinted with lengthy text. Fitton's poster was an early pre-war version of what was to become known as a *pair poster*.

To the Cinemas *Double royal poster*
CECIL WALTER BACON 1934

Bacon's decorative map clearly highlights the many West End cinemas, together with the main roads and Underground lines. Although he designed several posters for London Transport, he is best known for his illustrations for the *Radio Times*.

The Pictures *Press advertisement*
EDWARD BAWDEN 1928

The Underground made little profit if Londoners visited their local cinemas, which were probably within walking distance. This advertisement, which appeared in the *Evening News*, acknowledges the number of local cinemas. However, its main aim was to get people to catch films that much earlier by seeing them in the West End.

TO THE CINEMAS

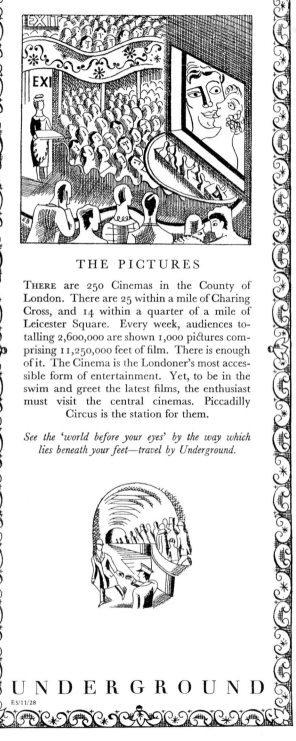

THE PICTURES

THERE are 250 Cinemas in the County of London. There are 25 within a mile of Charing Cross, and 14 within a quarter of a mile of Leicester Square. Every week, audiences totalling 2,600,000 are shown 1,000 pictures comprising 11,250,000 feet of film. There is enough of it. The Cinema is the Londoner's most accessible form of entertainment. Yet, to be in the swim and greet the latest films, the enthusiast must visit the central cinemas. Piccadilly Circus is the station for them.

See the 'world before your eyes' by the way which lies beneath your feet—travel by Underground.

UNDERGROUND

E3/11/28

Cheap Evening Return Fares
Double royal poster
TOM ECKERSLEY
and ERIC LOMBERS 1937

To encourage travel to central London in the evening, Cheap Evening Return tickets were introduced by London Transport. They were discontinued at the start of the Second World War and not reintroduced until 1953.

Summer Nights
Double royal poster
VLADIMIR POLUNIN 1930

The three pictures of people dining, dancing and visiting the theatre need no explanation. But very few people looking at this poster would identify the building as 55 Broadway, the then newly-completed head offices of the Underground.

Without television the only way to see the Boat Race, Wimbledon or Wembley Cup Final was to go and watch the event as it took place. Fortunately for the Underground the popularity of a wide range of mass spectator sports provided it with an ideal opportunity to promote off-peak travel. Most of the capital's main sporting venues were easily accessible by Underground. Of those which could not be reached directly by Underground, horse racing was the most notable. To get to watch the races at tracks such as Epsom and Sandown, Londoners had to use either the company's regular and special bus services or the overground railways.

Of all spectator sports the most important as regards attendance figures was football. In the London area there were 12 football clubs in the league whose home matches were watched by over seven million fans each season. Although the matches were held after the Saturday morning peak (Saturday for many Londoners was still then only a half holiday) they created

their own problems for the Underground with up to 45,000 passengers leaving a match at the same time. Other sports usually attracted fewer spectators. For instance, rugby in London, apart from the international matches held at Twickenham, had comparatively small attendances. The same applied to cricket, with only the international matches at the Oval or Lord's attracting large crowds. Nor did tennis attract crowds of spectators except during the two weeks of the Wimbledon championships when over 250,000 spectators attended the matches. Other spectator sports which attracted relatively large crowds included speedway, and both dog and horse racing.

The Underground did not just carry hordes of fans to a football or rugby match, it was also involved in transporting amateur sportsmen and women to some of the many sports grounds and playing fields dotted throughout the capital. There are no records of the numbers involved, but in 1930 sports grounds covered over 18,000 acres of land in London alone, and were planned to increase to 34,000 acres to meet the needs of Londoners. Although many people participated in recreational sports, they were of minor importance to the Underground and did not affect traffic flows as few passengers would have travelled at any one time to a specific destination. This is reflected in the small number of posters and other publicity issued to advertise these recreational sports, though the Underground did issue special tickets to Sports Clubs at a discounted rate.

For Football *Double royal poster*
S T C WEEKS 1913

This small poster was part of a set by Weeks, advertising the theatre, music and cathedrals. It is unusual in that it chooses to portray a goal keeper leaning against the goalpost, rather than the action and excitement to be found at most football matches.

Rugby League Cup Final
Panel poster
HERRY PERRY 1933

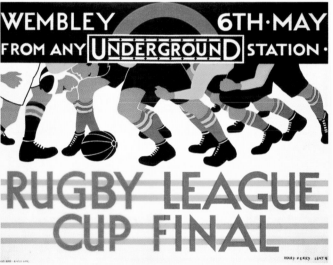

The Stand-off Half
Press advertisement
ANONYMOUS 1928

In 1928 the Underground issued a series of sporting press advertisements in which the player's role was explained to the reader.

THE STAND-OFF HALF.—Few, if any, players in a Rugby team are more important than the stand-off half, for largely upon him devolves the direction of attack and defence. Not only must he possess a safe pair of hands able to seize the ball from high or low passes, but he must have pace off the mark and an unerring eye for loopholes in the opposing defence. He must be 'on his toes' all through the game, for on the initial ground he makes directly he receives the ball depends the success of an attacking movement.

SEE YOUR 'RUGGER' AT TWICKENHAM AND BLACKHEATH

Travel to Twickenham by Underground to Hammersmith Station, and thence by London United Tramway Route 67.

Travel to Blackheath by 'General' Route 20 from Wood Green, 48 from Golder's Green, 54 from Plumstead and Croydon, or 108B from Bromley-by-Bow and Forest Hill.

E3/157/28

England versus Ireland
Double royal poster
CHARLES BURTON 1934

This poster appeared in at least one other version in which the text and colours of the players' shirts were changed to represent a match between branches of the armed forces.

ASSOCIATION FOOTBALL

FOR the 'Spurs'—book to Finsbury Park Station and travel thence by omnibus or tram to Tottenham; for the 'Pensioners'—book to Walham Green; for the 'Gunners'—book to Gillespie Road; for the 'Hammers'—book to Upton Park; for the 'Rangers'—book to Wood Lane or Shepherd's Bush; for the 'Lions'—book to New Cross Gate; for the 'Cottagers'—book to Putney Bridge; for the 'Bees'—book to South Ealing. The Grounds where these Teams play have capacities ranging from 25,000 to 80,000. Plenty of room for you.

Your favourites need your support.
Reach your goal by
Underground.

UNDERGROUND

E3/15/28

Cup Final *Panel poster*
TOM ECKERSLEY AND ERIC LOMBERS
1938

These small posters were the Underground's favourite way to promote sporting events. There was also the advantage that the Underground experimented with unknown artists in this smaller medium before allowing them to work on full size posters. Eckersley went on to become one of the Underground's most productive poster designers.

Association Football
Press advertisement
EDWARD BAWDEN 1928

Edward Bawden's long career for the Underground spanned over 45 years. In 1928 he designed a series of press advertisements to promote London's leisure attractions. So that he could accurately portray the subject for this advert, Bawden had to make a special visit to his first football match. He claimed he had never seen one before!

Cup Final *Panel poster*
ERIC FRASER 1926

When this poster was produced it was the Metropolitan Railway, not the Underground, that ran trains to Wembley Park, the nearest station to Wembley Stadium. The Bakerloo Line station at Wembley Central was a little further away. Retaining its independence until 1933, the Met also produced its own posters for this important sporting event. Fraser is, perhaps, best known for his illustrations in the *Radio Times*.

CUP FINAL WEMBLEY SATURDAY APRIL 24TH. FROM ANY UNDERGROUND STATION

Cup Final – May 1 *Panel poster*
G R MORRIS 1937

Morris's tongue in cheek look behind the scenes contrasts strongly with the more dramatic approach taken by both Fraser and Zinkeisen.

Cup Final *Panel poster*
ANNA ZINKEISEN 1934

In 1934 Anna Zinkeisen designed a series of 15 small panels for London Transport, covering a wide range of subjects from sport to London's parks and ceremonies. Each poster has a different style of bullseye, although all make some use of the Johnston typeface.

Lord's Oval *Double royal poster*
Andrew Power 1934

Lord's Oval *Double royal poster*
Andrew Power 1934

Matches held at Lord's and Oval grounds were the only cricket considered to be worthy of a pictorial poster. Although this poster is signed by 'Andrew Power', it was actually designed by a woman, Sybil Andrews. Both are the same person, but she used this *nom de pinceau* in recognition of the help she received from fellow artist Cyril Power in obtaining several commissions from London Transport.

LORD'S

ST. JOHNS WOOD STATION

BUS ROUTES: 2, 13, 48, 53, 74, 121, 153

MAY	MATCH
2, 3 & 4	M.C.C. v. Surrey
5, 7 & 8	M.C.C. v. Yorkshire
9, 10 & 11	MIDDLESEX v. Gloucestershire
12, 14 & 15	M.C.C. v. AUSTRALIANS
16, 17 & 18	MIDDLESEX v. Hampshire
19, 21 & 22	MIDDLESEX v. Sussex
23, 24 & 25	MIDDLESEX v. Somerset
26, 28 & 29	MIDDLESEX v. AUSTRALIANS
30, 31 & JUNE 1	MIDDLESEX v. Warwickshire

OVAL

OVAL STATION

BUS ROUTES: 3, 5, 36, 58, 59, 67, 133, 134, 136, 143, 159, 536

TRAM ROUTES: 2, 4, 6, 10, 16, 18, 22, 24, 33, 40, 54, 58, 72

MAY	MATCH
5, 7 & 8	SURREY v. Glamorgan
9, 10 & 11	SURREY v. Warwickshire
12, 14 & 15	SURREY v. Gloucestershire
30, 31 & JUNE 1	SURREY v. Australians

Lords – England *v* South Africa
Panel poster
Herry Perry 1935

In this colourful poster Perry has used two South African animals – a springbok and a lion – to represent South Africa and England.

First Test Match – Lords *Panel poster*
CLIFFORD and ROSEMARY ELLIS 1939

Third Test Match – The Oval *Panel poster*
CLIFFORD and ROSEMARY ELLIS 1939
Clifford and Rosemary Ellis were a husband and wife team who designed a number of posters for London Transport, including this pair of posters for test matches against the West Indies.

Epsom *Panel poster*
TOM ECKERSLEY AND ERIC LOMBERS
1938

There were no horse race courses directly accessible by Underground, so most of the company's publicity concentrated on its bus services. Today, it scarcely seems possible that the Underground would provide a bus every minute to connect with its Northern Line. However, on Derby Day in 1938 over 250,000 people flocked to Epsom, with 63,000 taking advantage of the special buses to and from Morden station.

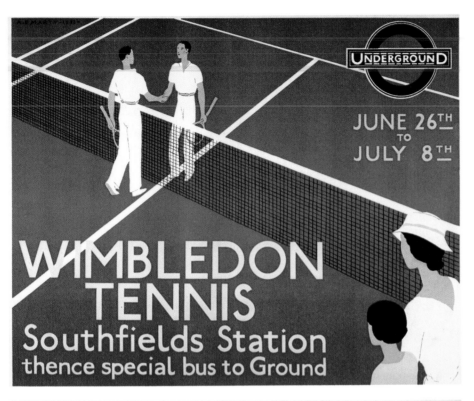

Wimbledon Tennis
Panel poster
A E Marty 1933

Wimbledon
Panel poster
Herry Perry 1931

In her poster of a mixed doubles match Perry has chosen to concentrate on the ballboy at the expense of the players.

Wimbledon *Double royal poster*
Andrew Power 1933

In 1933 the Underground issued two posters for Wimbledon fortnight. One, by Andrew Power, was intended to be displayed on platform and booking office walls and the other smaller one, by Marty, was for display inside carriages. Although advertising the same event, the style of each poster was completely different.

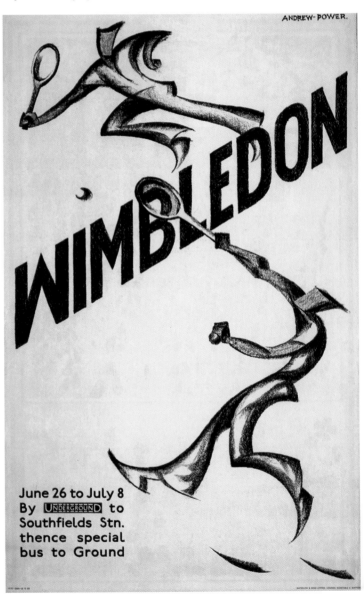

Davis Cup *Double royal poster*
TOM ECKERSLEY and ERIC LOMBERS
1935

The remarkable fact about this poster is that it was intended to be displayed only on the day preceding the match. It was then re-issued with different wording on the match day.

Davis Cup *Double royal poster*
TOM ECKERSLEY and ERIC LOMBERS
1937

The image on this poster was designed so that it could be used on double royal and panel posters with equal effect.

White City *Double royal poster*
CLIVE GARDINER 1927

With 22 greyhound racing tracks in London, the Underground concentrated its publicity on those best reached by its services. On some posters a blank space was left for the text to be overprinted or a sticker to be added. This had the advantage of allowing one image to be used with a variety of different messages, usually promoting different destinations.

I'm Going Underground
Panel poster
ALFRED LEETE 1928

This humorous poster of a surprised, or even terrified, hare being chased by a fierce looking dog, is a complete contrast to Gardiner's modernist poster of a year earlier. Yet in their different ways, both suggest movement. Leete is best known for his wartime poster *Your Country Needs You*.

Six-Day Cycle Race *Panel poster*
BEATH (JOHN M FLEMING) 1936

In the 1930s several small panel posters were issued to advertise the annual Cycle and Motor Cycle shows held at Olympia. However, this is the only London Transport poster issued to advertise a cycle race.

Ice Rinks *Double royal poster*
TOM ECKERSLEY AND ERIC LOMBERS
1935

The decorative element across the top of the poster is enough to catch the eye but does not distract from the large amount of detailed text to be found beneath it.

Empress Hall *Panel poster*
WALTER GOETZ 1937

Most of the Underground's sporting posters advertised mass spectator sports. As well as advertising ice hockey, which had recently become popular, Goetz's poster also encourages passengers to go ice skating themselves.

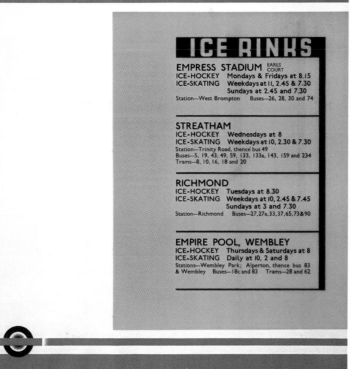

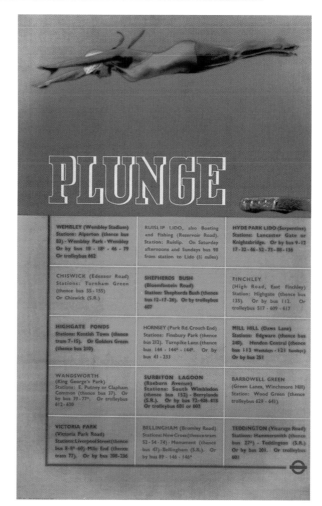

Plunge *Double royal poster*
ANONYMOUS 1938

By 1938 a London County Council building programme resulted in 17 open air swimming pools and lakes being available for Londoners, many of which are listed on this poster. It was hoped that once the image of the diver had arrested the eye, the waiting passenger would want to read the text.

OPEN AIR LONDON

To Regent's Park *Double royal poster*
DORA M BATTY 1932

Many of London's parks were noted for their flower displays. This 1932 poster advertises the new Rose Garden at Regent's Park, which opened in that year and replaced the Royal Botanical Society's gardens which had stood there since 1839.

"The parks are one of London's glories. Foreign visitors are enchanted by the green expanse which stretches from St James's Park to Kensington Gardens. No other European capital has anything like this in such a central position." These words form the introduction to a book *Open-Air London* published jointly by London Transport and the London County Council in 1939. London has always been fortunate in the number and diversity of its parks. Many, such as St James's Park, originated as royal parks or hunting grounds. Others were originally the private gardens or estates of large houses, Osterley and Kenwood being examples. As London continued to expand at an alarming rate, rapidly devouring the countryside around it, her parks became crucial in providing Londoners with open space. In the 1920s and 1930s the London County Council saw the development of existing parks and the creation of new parks as instrumental in improving the lifestyle of people living in London.

Visiting London did not necessarily involve shopping, or museums and galleries. If the weather was fine there was always much to see and do in the parks. In central London, many of the parks were major attractions in their own right, with bandstands, a lido and even horse riding available, while others, notably Green Park, featured rarely if at all, on Underground posters. The Underground did not just confine itself to advertising these central parks but also issued regular posters promoting the delights of Kew Gardens, Richmond Park and Hampstead Heath, all of which were easily accessible by Underground train.

Every spring and summer the Underground's publicity department began another campaign of posters, leaflets and press advertisements, exhorting Londoners and visitors to relax in the parks. Artists were quick to spot that nature continually provided something new to be seen throughout the year. The Underground regularly marketed a whole variety of *seasons* on its posters. These included crocus time, followed by bluebell time, daffodil time, Chestnut Sunday, blackberry time and even harvest time. Rarely did the Underground produce a single series of posters to be displayed throughout the whole year. However, in 1911 a series of 12 panel posters by T. R. Way were issued at the rate of one a month to show the attractions of the changing seasons to be found at Kew Gardens. Although greater London had thousands of acres of open space, parks and gardens were not the only outdoor attractions. There was the Thames (covered in another chapter), famous sights such as Trafalgar Square, Piccadilly Circus, Big Ben and Buckingham Palace, and regular outdoor events including the popular flying displays at Hendon.

St James's Park *Double royal poster*
EDWARD BAWDEN 1936

This poster was also used to
advertise Regent's Park and Hyde
Park. The cheapest way to advertise
several destinations on different
posters was to commission one
design and later add the relevant
wording to the poster. This was only
possible when the lettering, here in
Johnston type, was not an integral
part of the design.

Kensington Gardens
Double royal poster
MRS G BARRACLOUGH 1923

In 1923 the Underground issued
two posters of Kensington Gardens,
both linking the park to the fictional
character Peter Pan. This poster by
Mrs Barraclough was one of a pair,
with the other by her showing
Regent's Park.

Snatch Summer's Closing Days
Panel poster
DORA M BATTY 1927

These elegant panels by Batty portray the changing seasons of London's parks and countryside. In each poster Batty has kept to the single theme of a woman admiring the season's flowers to produce an attractive series. It seems odd that, if these panels were intended to be seen as a unified series, different styles of lettering were used, some in Johnston, others in a flowing script. Two of the posters do not even mention travel by either Underground or bus.

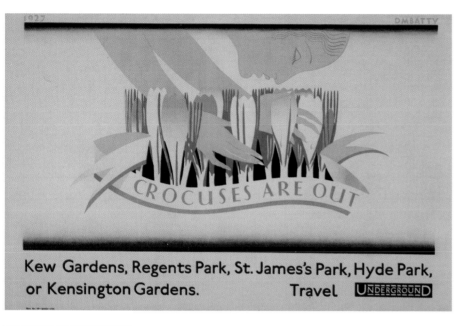

Crocuses are Out *Panel poster*
Dora M Batty 1927

Daffodils are Blooming *Panel poster*
Dora M Batty 1927

Come Out and See It *Panel poster*
Dora M Batty 1927

See London's Gardens *Panel poster*
Dora M Batty 1927

HYDE PARK

For Swimming, Sun-Bathing, Boating, Golf, Arguments, and Music (every afternoon and evening except Thursday afternoon). See the new Bowling Green and miniature Golf Course!

TRAVEL **UNDERGROUND** TO HYDE PARK CORNER STATION

M3/86n/51

Hyde Park *Press advertisement*
ANONYMOUS 1931

Hyde Park *Double royal poster*
EDWARD BAWDEN 1925

Hyde Park had the widest range of attractions available in a central London Park, with most of them listed on this press advertisement. 'Arguments' refers not to the domestic kind, but to the lively debates which could be found at Speakers' Corner. Both press advertisement and poster depict Rotten Row, the only space devoted to horse riding in central London.

Bands in the Parks
Press advertisement
ALTHEA WILLOUGHBY 1934

Bandstands were popular in many of London's Parks, with regular concerts held during the summer months. Following the formation of London Transport, several press advertisements had borders made from the repeated letters 'LT' to several different designs.

Richmond Park *Double royal poster*
ANONYMOUS 1908

This very traditional poster of
Richmond was typical of a number
of posters produced at the time by
the Underground. Although part of
the Underground since 1902, the
District Railway was often still
marketed under its own name until
1933.

Cheap Return Fare to Kew Gardens or Richmond
Double royal poster
AUSTIN COOPER 1929

Cooper produced a series of posters, similar to this,
advertising Cheap Return Fares to a variety of
stations. A master of the airbrush, Cooper makes good
use of this technique in this striking graphic poster.
Unlike other posters, no attempt is made by way of
amusing copy or seductive image to suggest why the
passenger would wish to travel to Kew or Richmond.

Dahlias in the Parks
Double royal poster
JOHN MANSBRIDGE 1934

Flowers of the brightly coloured
dahlia family appear to have been
particularly popular at the time of
this poster, which shows some of the
varieties to bear the name.

Special Shows of Dahlias
Double royal poster
DORA M BATTY 1935

In 1934 and 1935 six posters in this
style were designed by Batty
advertising the different floral
displays to be found in London's
parks.

The Palm House, Kew Gardens
Double royal poster
CLIVE GARDINER 1926

Along with London Zoo, Kew
Gardens appeared on more
Underground and London
Transport posters than any other
destination. Clive Gardiner
designed 27 posters for the
combine, many in a cubist or
modernist style.

GOLDERS HILL PARK

BY TRAIN TO GOLDERS GREEN

CHEAP RETURN TICKETS ON SUNDAYS AND BANK HOLIDAYS.

Golders Hill Park *Leaflet*
ANONYMOUS c1912

Until the arrival of the Underground in 1907, Golders Green was undeveloped countryside. In the next few years there was a dramatic increase in the population, leaving only the attractive Golders Hill Park as open space.

Golders Green *Double royal poster*
ANONYMOUS 1908

This early example of a poster using the new house style was also adapted as a leaflet, giving train times and fares to Golders Green.

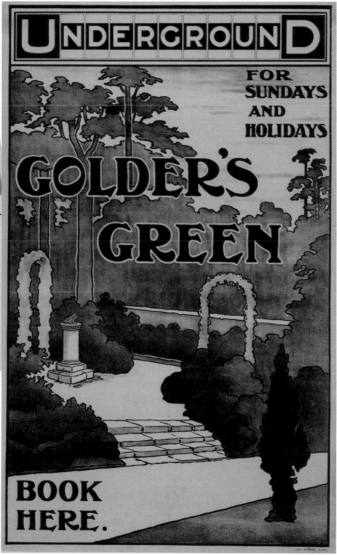

Hampstead *Postcard*
ANONYMOUS c1915

The message on this postcard is very clear: take the Underground to Hampstead. On the reverse is a table listing the fares from a selection of Underground stations to Hampstead and Golders Green. When this card was issued the single fare from Charing Cross to Hampstead was 3d (1.25p) or 5d (2p) for a Cheap Sunday Return.

Scenes along the Hampstead Tube *Postcard*
ANONYMOUS c1908

In its early days the Underground issued sets of postcards highlighting places of interest to be found along its routes. Similar cards were issued by the Bakerloo and Piccadilly Tubes.

Kenwood – London's New Park
Double royal poster
WALTER E SPRADBERY 1925

For Hampstead Heath
Double royal poster
WALTER E SPRADBERY 1912

Spradbery was a prolific artist designing 80 posters for the Underground and London Transport between 1912 and 1944. This was his first poster.

In 1922 the Kenwood Preservation Council bought most of the estate and presented it to the London County Council in 1924. It was opened to the public by King George V in 1925. Spradbery's poster captures the rural beauty of London's new park next to Hampstead Heath.

**See the Iveagh Bequest
at Ken Wood** *Panel poster*
J BETTS 1928

In 1927 the First Earl of Iveagh
bequeathed the remainder of the
park, together with Kenwood
House and his art collection, to the
nation. This small decorative map,
issued as a panel to be posted inside

carriages, commemorates this new
bequest and clearly shows its
relationship to the original public
spaces and the local bus and
Underground links.

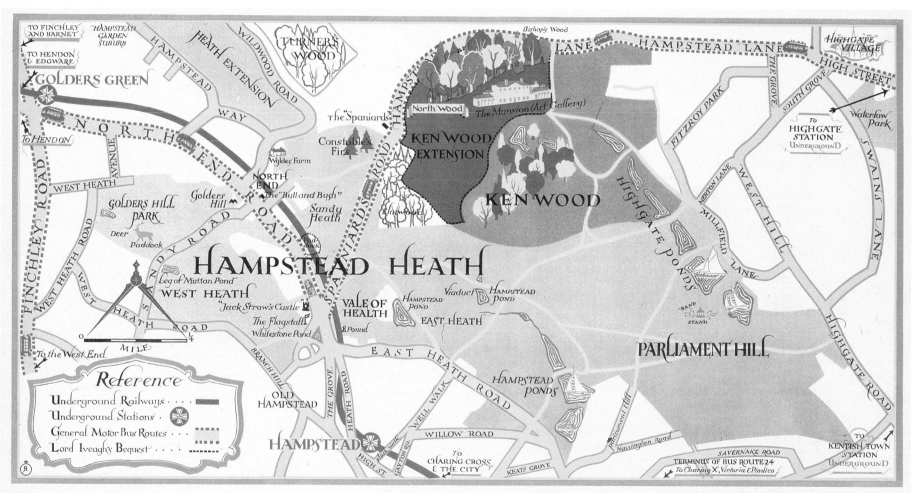

SEE THE IVEAGH BEQUEST AT KEN WOOD
NOW OPEN

Chestnut Sunday *Panel poster*
EDWARD BAWDEN 1936

Bushy Park was famed for its mile long Chestnut Avenue and for several years the Underground produced an annual poster to encourage the public to visit the trees on Chestnut Sunday when they were in full blossom.

Chestnut Sunday *Panel poster*
ANNA K ZINKEISEN 1934

Chestnut Sunday *Panel poster*
BETTY SWANWICK 1937

Chestnut Sunday *Panel poster*
A E MARTY 1933

Chestnut Sunday *Panel poster*
HERRY PERRY 1935

Bluebell Time *Panel poster*
A E MARTY 1933

Bluebell Time *Panel poster*
HERRY PERRY 1931

Herry Perry's panel poster does not
mention the Underground at all.
There is not even a bullseye to
identify it as publicity for the
undertaking. Its display inside
Underground trains was perhaps
sufficient.

A DAY IN TOWN

Cheap Day Return to Town
Double royal poster
F GREGORY BROWN 1932

In this poster the artist has used the
image of a boomerang to suggest
the idea of a return journey linking
Eros, the heart of the city, to a
typical suburban house.

Central London provided a wide
variety of indoor attractions for
both Londoners and people living
out of town. There was never a
shortage of things to see and do,
whether it was a visit to the Tower
of London or Kensington Palace;
an annual event, such as the
dogs show at Crufts, or the
Smithfield Cattle Show in
Islington, or even one of the
many regularly changing
exhibitions at the 39 museums
and galleries which could be
found throughout London.
The Underground did not
simply issue posters to
promote, say, the National
Gallery or Science Museum,
but also issued posters to
announce temporary
exhibitions as diverse as
'Television' or 'Smoke
Abatement', both at the Science
Museum. This must have been an invaluable form of free
advertising for the institutions concerned.

In 1936 just over 1.3 million people visited the British
Museum, compared with 6.7 million today. Nearly as many
visited the Science Museum, while the Natural History
Museum, Victoria & Albert Museum and National Gallery
each drew between half and three quarters of a million
visitors. Other important sights included the Tower of
London, Hampton Court, the Imperial Institute and
Madame Tussauds. Two factors tended to govern which

venues the Underground chose to advertise: accessibility to
an Underground line and popularity of the attraction. Only
occasionally would less well known galleries and museums,
such as Hogarth's House or the Horniman Museum be
advertised. However during the 1920s and 1930s, the most
important attraction by far was London Zoo with nearly two
million visitors a year and this was reflected in the number of
posters issued.

While pictorial posters, with their bright and colourful
images, were the main form of publicity created by the
Underground to encourage people to use its services, they
were not its only publicity. Following the lead set in London
by the District Railway, the Underground published guide
books detailing many of the unusual tourist attractions to be
found in the capital. One such series of seven guides
published in the late 1930s included titles such as 'London
Craftsmen' which pinpointed some of the curiosities to be
found in many of London's museums, and 'Serious
Pleasures' which was described by *The Times Literary
Supplement* as "A stimulating picture of London as a
dispenser of democratic culture". This popular and
interesting series would doubtless have been extended had it
not been for the outbreak of the Second World War.

Whether in guidebooks or on posters it was not just
London's many museums that were advertised. Frequent
exhibitions were held in the booking hall of Charing Cross
Underground station and these were regularly promoted by
the company's posters. The Underground clearly saw its role
as playing an important part in the social fabric of the capital,
not merely transporting passengers. Its publicity advertising
the wide range of attractions in London did much more than
just promote travel to these institutions, it also promoted
London itself as a lively, educated and cultural city.

The Royal Tournament *Panel poster*
HERRY PERRY 1931

The Royal Tournament *Panel poster*
A E MARTY 1933

One of London's major annual events,
the Royal Tournament was first staged in 1880 at the
Royal Horticultural Hall, Islington, transferring to
Earl's Court some years later. Between 1923 and 1939
the Underground issued an annual panel poster to
advertise the Tournament at Earl's Court, which has
remained its home ever since.

Smithfield Club Cattle Show
Panel poster
BETTY SWANWICK 1936

Livestock and other animal
exhibitions were held at the Royal
Agricultural Hall between 1861 and
1939, when the hall closed. London
Transport issued panel posters
advertising the cattle and dairy
shows between 1927 and 1938.

Smithfield Club Show *Panel poster*
COMPTON BENNETT 1928

Although Angel station is clearly
recognisable in this poster, the
platforms, shown here as wide and
spacious, were in truth narrow and
unable to cope with large crowds.
The whole station was rebuilt in
1992. Note that the poster on the
wall also advertises the Smithfield
Cattle Show.

Motor Show *Panel poster*
A E MARTY 1933

Although motoring was still not available to the masses, the Motor Show was a popular attraction with over a quarter of a million people attending it during the ten days that it was open. This stylish poster by Marty captures the pleasures of pre-war motoring along empty country roads. The building on the horizon is the Olympia exhibition centre.

Motor Show
Panel and double royal posters
EDWARD MCKNIGHT KAUFFER 1937

In 1937 Kauffer was asked to produce two posters for the Motor Show, one to appear on the stations and the other inside the Underground cars. Kauffer preferred not to use Johnston typeface on his posters, instead designing his own lettering which formed an intrinsic part of his poster design.

Smoke Abatement
Double royal poster
BEATH (MYLES FLEMING) 1936

Smoke pollution, the subject of this simple but effective poster, was a major problem in cities until post-war Clean Air legislation.

Clear the Air *Double royal poster*
ANONYMOUS 1938

For many years exhibitions were held in the ticket hall at Charing Cross Underground station. Simple photographic montages, such as seen in this poster, were used to produce an effective and striking design.

SMOKE ABATEMENT
an Exhibition in the Science Museum
from October 2 - 31 admission free
open weekdays 10-6 · Sundays 2.30-6
nearest station South Kensington

AN EXHIBITION PRESENTED BY THE GAS LIGHT AND COKE COMPANY FOR THE
NATIONAL SMOKE ABATEMENT SOCIETY
CHARING X UNDERGROUND
STATION TICKET HALL
NOVEMBER 28 TO DECEMBER 15
OPEN ALL DAY

Atlantic Steam Navigation Centenary Exhibition
Double royal poster
ANONYMOUS 1938

The centenary referred to in this poster was not that of the first steamship to cross the Atlantic in 1819, but the race between the Sirius and the Great Western in 1838 – the start of rapid and reliable transatlantic travel.

Television *Double royal poster*
ANONYMOUS 1937

The BBC began its first regular television broadcasts in November 1936, so when the Science Museum held this exhibition, television would still have been a new experience to most people.

Imperial Institute
Double royal poster
ANONYMOUS 1938

Demolished in the early 1960s, the Imperial Institute was not just home to exhibitions of the British Empire, but also housed the Imperial War Museum from 1924 until it moved to its present home at Lambeth in 1936. The only part of the building to remain is the tower, which can be clearly seen in this poster.

Cathedral Church of St Saviour, Southwark
Double royal poster
CHARLES PEARS 1932

The 13th century Southwark Cathedral, less famous than St Paul's Cathedral or Westminster Abbey, is situated in a less prosperous part of London, south of the River and off the tourist track. Charles Pears produced a number of posters depicting the interior of London's churches. A keen lithographer, he often preferred to draw directly onto the stone rather than have his illustrations copied by the printers' lithographer, which was the usual method.

Westminster Abbey *Panel poster*
EDWARD McKNIGHT KAUFFER 1936

This poster, one of a set advertising Westminster, Buckingham Palace and The Tower, was originally printed as a double royal size poster two years earlier.

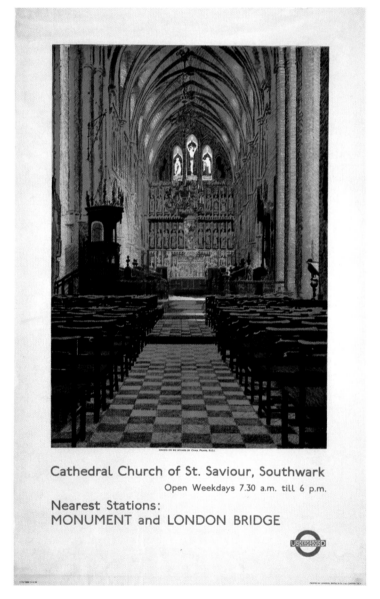

Cathedral Church of St. Saviour, Southwark
Open Weekdays 7.30 a.m. till 6 p.m.

Nearest Stations:
MONUMENT and LONDON BRIDGE

WESTMINSTER ABBEY

Natural History Museum
Double royal poster
EDWARD BAWDEN 1925

This was the first poster which Bawden designed for the Underground without help. It is unusual in that it is an early example of silk screen printing.

The Rocket at the Science Museum
Double royal poster
EDWARD MCKNIGHT KAUFFER 1923

This poster showing Stephenson's *Rocket* marked the re-opening of the Land Transport Galleries at the Science Museum in 1923. In that year the Underground presented to the Science Museum its first electric locomotive which had been built for the City & South London Railway.

WHO SAYS
'LONDON'S DULL
ON SUNDAY'?

Amuse yourself among the birds, beasts and fishes of this very wonderful World at the Natural History Museum (open from 2 p.m. to 6 p.m.).

Book to South Kensington Station by
UNDERGROUND

Who says 'London's Dull on Sunday'? *Press advertisement*
ARTHUR WATTS 1928

This is one of a series of press advertisements by Arthur Watts, in which the public were encouraged to visit the many attractions open on Sunday.

OPEN FREE DAILY
MARCH to SEPT.
10 – 6
SUNDAYS
2.30 – 6

OCTOBER to FEB.
10 – 5
SUNDAYS
2.30 – 6

Natural History Museum

NEAREST STATION
SOUTH KENSINGTON

THE "ROCKET" OF MR. STEPHENSON
OF NEWCASTLE
1829

AT THE
MUSEUM
OF SCIENCE
SOUTH KENSINGTON

**Ceramics at
the Victoria & Albert
Museum**

**Antiquities at
the British Museum**

**Objects d'Art
– Wallace Collection**

**Souvenirs
– Imperial War Museum**

Double royal posters
Austin Cooper 1932

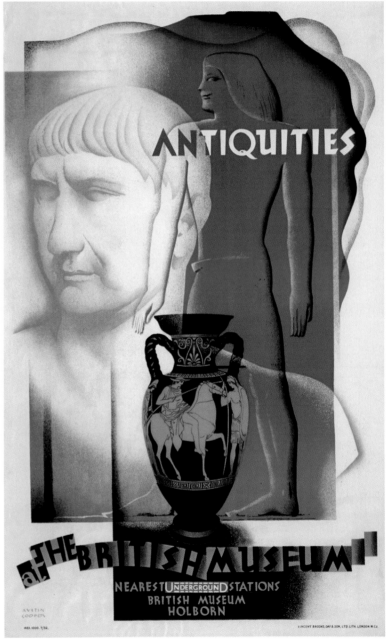

Cooper, noted for his use of the air-brush, was one of the best paid commercial artists of his day. He produced over 54 posters for the Underground. These four posters were the second set he designed for the Underground in which the attractions of London's museums were depicted. In 1936, four years after the date of these posters, the Imperial War Museum moved from South Kensington to its present home at Lambeth.

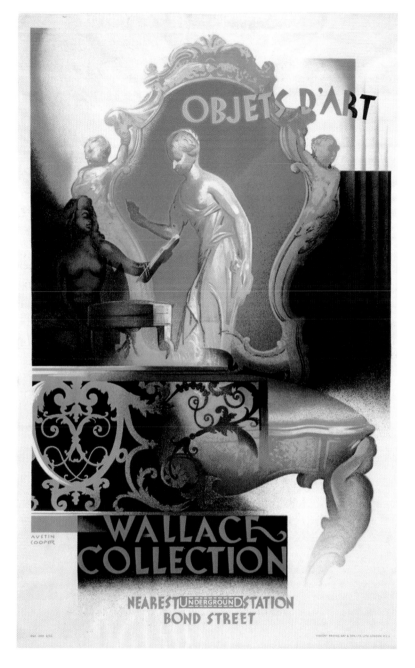

London's Leisure Hours
Double royal posters
AUSTIN COOPER 1933

One of a series of four posters by Cooper, each advertising different types of attractions to be found throughout London. While this poster promoted Underground travel, the others in the series were issued for travel by the company's other operations, namely bus, tram and coach.

Visit the Tower

Visit Kensington Palace
Double royal posters
DORA M BATTY 1938

These posters of two of London's Palaces, one a major tourist attraction, the other still a royal home, use images of their most famous residents, the two Princes in the Tower and a young Princess Victoria, rather than views of the buildings to suggest the subjects. Although obviously a pair, with similar lettering, the style of bullseye used is quite different on each poster.

"There's a
Transport of Joy at the Zoo."

LPTB

Camden Town, Chalk Farm or
Regents Park "Underground" Stn.

"There's a Transport of Joy at the Zoo" *Double royal poster*
JEAN DUPAS 1933

Once again, this poster is part of a set of four promoting the different modes of transport offered by the newly formed London Passenger Transport Board.

New Aquarium Now Open
Double royal poster
GEORGE SHERINGHAM 1924

When London Zoo's aquarium opened in 1924 it was a major event and honoured with two Underground posters. In subsequent years the Underground would often issue two posters, one for the Zoo and the other devoted to the aquarium.

THE ZOO'S AQUARIUM

THE NEW AQUARIUM
NOW OPEN
Book to
REGENT'S PARK
or CAMDEN TOWN
UNDERGROUND

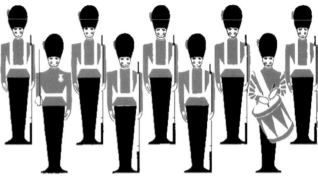

Royal, state and civic ceremonies have, for many years, provided Londoners with a popular form of free entertainment. As the capital of the United Kingdom, and also of empire, London regularly played host to a large variety of state and civic occasions. Some ceremonies were semi-private events; many were much more than just a matter of state. They were also major public attractions taking place in the heart of the city. Of particular note are two annual events – Trooping the Colour, which has been regularly performed since 1805, and the Lord Mayor's Show whose origins date from 1215. These were popular and have always attracted large crowds. Other events, which automatically warranted the attention of the Underground's poster artists, were coronations and royal weddings.

Processions and parades through London's streets provided the Underground with the opportunity to increase its patronage by carrying spectators to see them. For a major event the Underground's posters and leaflets would serve two purposes – to maximise the number of passengers by publicising the event and to advise travellers that road services may be disrupted while it was on. Because the railways had their tracks to themselves they were able to take people speedily to the best and closest viewing positions in the heart of the city.

Most of these events were advertised by the same means as other spectaculars, such as the Boat Race and Wimbledon Fortnight – usually by the use of small posters on the draught screens inside the carriages. The main purpose of these posters was to tell existing passengers what they could see happening in their city, particularly by travelling during off-peak times. Occasionally the Underground might also have had another purpose. Some events were of national significance and the Underground saw them not just as a marketing opportunity, but also as demonstrating its patriotism by showing, for example, its support for the royal family. This patriotic, or propaganda role, was naturally most prominent during the two world wars, when many of its posters were less concerned with promoting pleasure travel than with concise public information and propaganda.

AT THE HORSEGUARDS
WHITEHALL
at 11a.m (Sundays at 10 a.m.)
Nearest Stations:—
Westminster and Trafalgar Square.

AT BUCKINGHAM PALACE or
ST JAMES'S PALACE
between 10·30 and 11·15 a.m.
Nearest Stations:—
St James's Park and Dover Street.

CHANGING THE GUARD
LONDON'S DAILY MILITARY TATTOOS

UNDERGROUND

Changing the Guard
Double royal poster
EDWARD BAWDEN 1925

Considering its popularity with Londoners and tourists alike, it is surprising that this appears to be the only pictorial poster to advertise this daily ceremonial event, held in the heart of the capital.

Jubilee Week in London *Double royal poster*
HAROLD STABLER 1935

The Underground issued a series of 15 posters designed by Harold Stabler to commemorate the Silver Jubilee of King George V. With the exception of the poster depicting the royal coat of arms, all the posters used an identical design, with different text overprinted in Johnston typeface. It is clear from this poster that the Underground used the celebrations as an excuse to promote a wide variety of attractions, not all of which were connected with the Jubilee.

Silver Jubilee *Panel poster*
IRENE FAWKES 1935

It is unclear why the Underground used Fawkes' design to appear inside its trains when the main work had been given to Harold Stabler. The only reason might be that Fawkes' design was used on other publicity commemorating the event.

The success of Stabler's Jubilee posters led to a further commission to produce another set for the Coronation of King George VI. This set followed a similar pattern to the 1935 posters, with one showing the crown and another design which could be overprinted to list all the special events.

Coronation Day 12 May
Double royal poster
HAROLD STABLER 1937

Coronation Arrangements Folder
Double royal poster
HAROLD STABLER 1937

The Royal Wedding
Double royal poster
DORA M BATTY 1934/5

Royal weddings were popular events, with the processions to church attracting large crowds.

National Reserve – London Division *Double royal poster*
CHARLES SHARLAND 1912

Territorial Review
Double royal poster
CHARLES SHARLAND 1913

In the years preceding the First World War, several posters were issued to encourage travel to military and naval reviews held in Hyde Park and along the river.

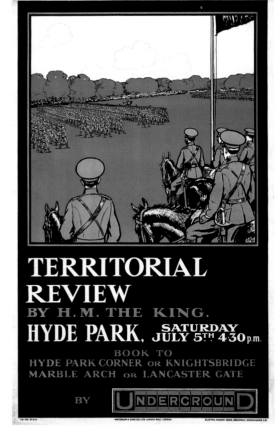

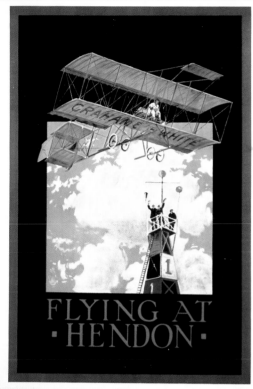

Flying at Hendon *Double royal poster*
TONY SARG 1913

When Hendon Aerodrome opened it was one of the earliest in London and aeroplanes were still a novelty. Situated in the countryside just outside urban London, it was necessary to complete the journey by bus as Golders Green was then the terminus of the Charing Cross Euston & Hampstead Railway.

RAF Display *Panel poster*
ANONYMOUS 1927

Between 1920 and 1937 the Air Ministry held annual aerial displays at Hendon, which attracted over 100,000 visitors each year. With the opening, in 1924, of the extension from Golders Green to Colindale, on what is now the Northern Line, it became possible to travel directly to the aerodrome by Underground.

RAF Display *Panel poster*
A E MARTY 1933

RAF Pageant *Panel poster*
MIDDLETON 1937

1937 was the last year in which the annual RAF Display was held at Hendon, as aircraft were becoming too big and fast for the limited space at the aerodrome.

To Hampstead, Nov 5TH
Double royal poster
CHARLES SHARLAND 1912

In 1910, 1911 and 1912 the Underground advertised the Guy Fawkes celebrations on Hampstead Heath.

State Opening of Parliament
Double royal poster
ANONYMOUS 1913

Few pictorial posters have been issued for the State Opening of Parliament. This poster, showing crowds lining the route of the procession, was originally printed without the green text, enabling the design to be used more than once.

H M The King Reviews the Police
Double royal poster
ANONYMOUS 1935

The truncheons, as part of the motif, were an odd choice since they were not normally seen by law abiding citizens. Unless another poster gave more warning, one day's notice of this event gives little time for people to make arrangements to go.

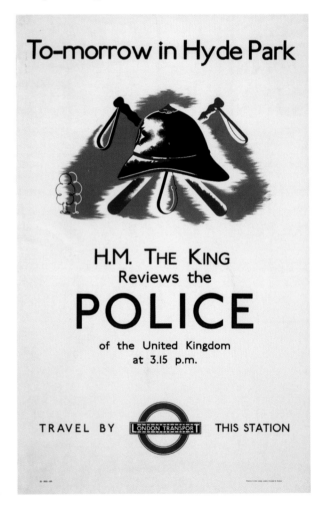

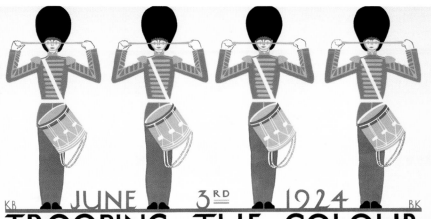

Trooping the Colour *Panel poster*
ALDO COSOMATI 1923

Trooping the Colour *Panel poster*
KATE BURRELL 1924

The Underground used small panel posters inside the trains to advertise many ceremonial events. These panels were printed in far larger numbers than the standard poster sizes which appeared at the stations.

Lord Mayor's Show *Panel poster*
HAL MISSINGHAM 1936

Most posters portrayed the Lord Mayor's coach, which is now kept on display in the Museum of London. The Lord Mayor used to ride astride a horse until 1711, when Sir George Heathcote was thrown from his. Lord Mayors have since greeted the onlookers from within a coach.

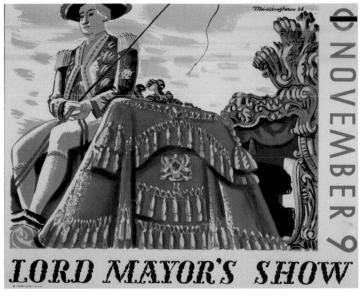

Lord Mayor's Show
Double royal poster
CHARLES SHARLAND 1913

A major annual event in the City of London is the Lord Mayor's Show which, to this day, usually merits a poster. In 1913 the crowds that it attracted led to a 10 per cent increase in passengers on the Underground on the day of the event.

Lord Mayor's Show *Panel poster*
EDWARD WADSWORTH 1936

Although Wadsworth's design was printed, it may not have been used, the image of the guns being too brutal. This may well explain why Missingham's poster was also printed that year.

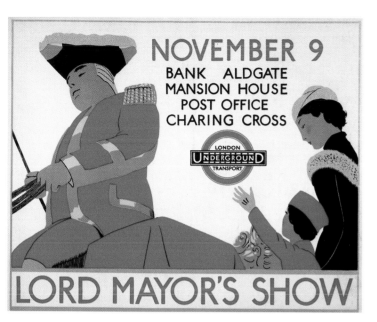

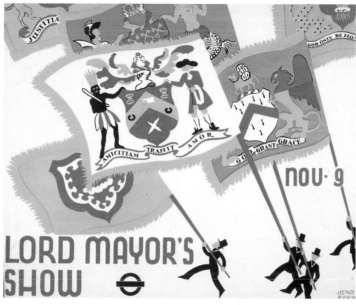

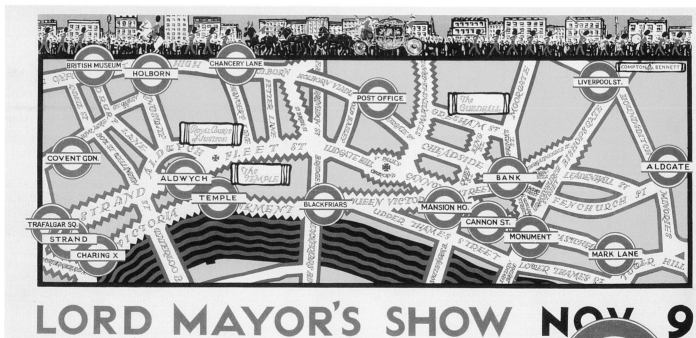

This map, showing the route of the procession, appeared inside the Underground carriages and gave much more useful information than the majority of posters advertising the event. Often posters only gave the date of the show and failed to name the nearest Underground stations.

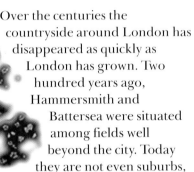

LONDON'S COUNTRY

Book to Perivale *Double royal poster*
CHARLES SHARLAND 1909
Now, almost 80 years after this poster was issued, it would be impossible to find the *field-path ramble in old-fashioned country* in the little that remains of the once extensive countryside near Perivale, Sudbury or Harrow.

Over the centuries the countryside around London has disappeared as quickly as London has grown. Two hundred years ago, Hammersmith and Battersea were situated among fields well beyond the city. Today they are not even suburbs, but are part of the central area, while the suburbs stretch ever further afield swallowing up whole villages and towns as they go. Little, if any, of once rural Middlesex has escaped the urban sprawl and large parts of Kent and Surrey where they approach London have also been engulfed by development.

It is difficult, therefore, to be consistent in defining London's countryside. What may be shown as rural in an early poster might, 30 or 40 years later, be no more than a new housing development with, perhaps, a small vestige of the once extensive green lanscape remaining in the form of a suburban park or heath.

In the early posters Golders Green, Pinner, Wimbledon and Hounslow were still rural enough for the Underground's publicity department to promote them as countryside, but by the 1930s development was already encroaching, leaving only a few open spaces amongst the new houses. Areas such as Kenwood, near Hampstead Heath, were saved from development and promoted as parks but others such as Hounslow Heath were quickly disappearing under tarmac. The creation of the Green Belt around London finally put paid to the worst excesses of London's urban sprawl.

The countryside around London has always been a magnet attracting Londoners keen to escape the urban grime. From almost its earliest days the Underground took advantage of this desire for nature and the open air by publicising the merits of its own rail and bus services. With the exception of the District Railway, the Underground did not extend much beyond the suburbs until it took control of the Metropolitan Railway in 1933, which put places as far away as Aylesbury and Amersham directly onto the Underground system.

Ironically the Underground, designed primarily as a commuter railway, was partially responsible for the destruction of the very landscape that its posters promoted. Wherever a new line was built development soon followed, pushing the countryside still further from London. Without the ever-expanding tube railways, development would still have taken place around London, but it would have taken a different pattern. Today, it is almost impossible to imagine Hounslow Heath (now Heathrow Airport) or Perivale as the pleasant countryside they are shown to be in the posters.

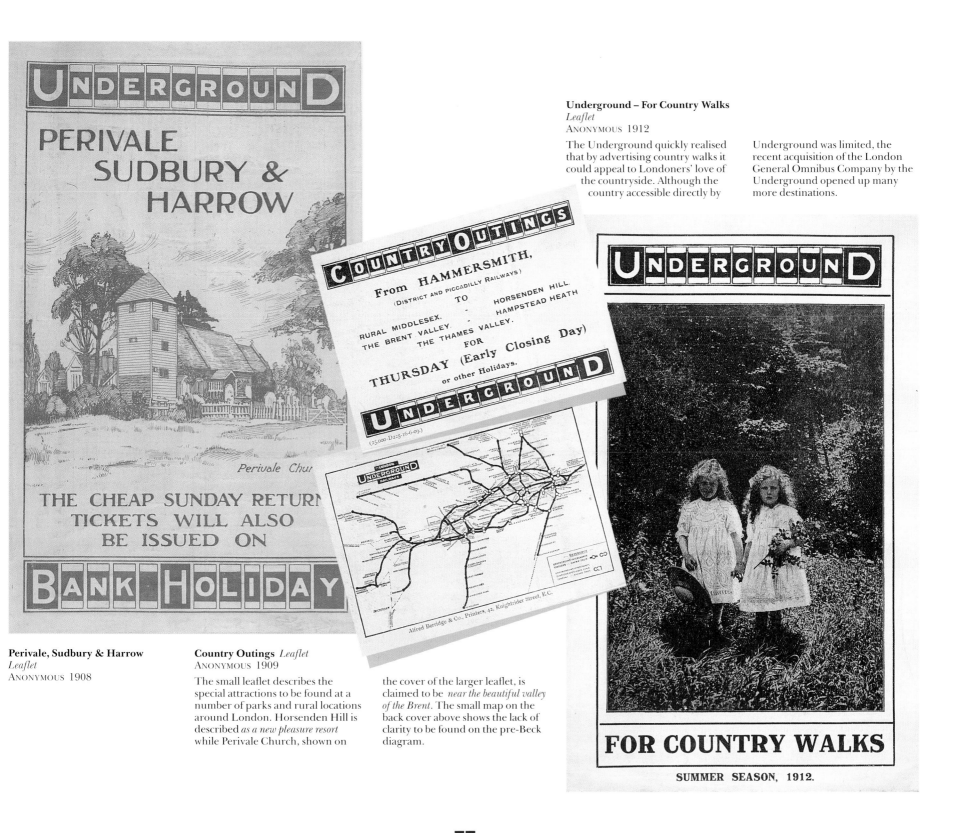

Underground – For Country Walks
Leaflet
ANONYMOUS 1912

The Underground quickly realised that by advertising country walks it could appeal to Londoners' love of the countryside. Although the country accessible directly by Underground was limited, the recent acquisition of the London General Omnibus Company by the Underground opened up many more destinations.

Perivale, Sudbury & Harrow
Leaflet
ANONYMOUS 1908

Country Outings *Leaflet*
ANONYMOUS 1909

The small leaflet describes the special attractions to be found at a number of parks and rural locations around London. Horsenden Hill is described *as a new pleasure resort* while Perivale Church, shown on the cover of the larger leaflet, is claimed to be *near the beautiful valley of the Brent*. The small map on the back cover above shows the lack of clarity to be found on the pre-Beck diagram.

Book to Ruislip
Double royal poster
R Stiles 1912

This was Stiles's second and last poster for the Underground. Both advertised 'Ruislip' as though it were deep in the countryside, with the earlier poster describing the area as 'Wooded Middlesex'.

Easy Walks from Uxbridge Station
Double royal poster
John Henry Lloyd 1911

On 1 March 1910 the District Railway extended from South Harrow to Rayners Lane and then over the Metropolitan Railway's tracks to Uxbridge. In addition, trams of the Underground Group (London United Tramways) also ran between west London and Uxbridge. Uxbridge could be reached more quickly by way of the Metropolitan Railway, although no mention was made on Underground posters as it was not part of the 'combine'.

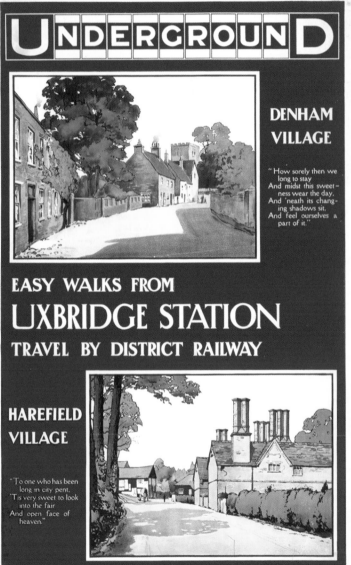

By Underground into the Country *Double royal landscape poster*
ANONYMOUS 1910

This could have been a poster advertising a District Railway destination, had
it not been for the inclusion of Golders Green which, until the line was
extended in 1923, was the terminus of the Charing Cross Euston &
Hampstead Railway – *the Hampstead Tube*. This scene is still theoretically
possible at Osterley Park and Wimbledon Common – the rest is now deep
within suburbia.

Pinner by District Railway
Double royal poster
NANCY SMITH 1916

In common with most of the posters produced by the Underground during the First World War, the conflict is completely ignored. While the main line railways were given a government subsidy to turn over their services to wartime essentials, the Underground was not. It had to consider first its ability to pay its way by generating any extra custom that it could.

Whitsuntide in the Country
Quad royal poster
EDWARD MCKNIGHT KAUFFER 1925

Kauffer was the Underground's leading poster designer, but surprisingly he only ever designed one quad royal poster for display at stations. This poster is unusual in that it was designed either to appear by itself, or as a central panel of a triptych. All three posters were issued in two versions advertising either Whitsun or summer.

Autumn in Country
Double royal poster
T R WAY 1912

Wimbledon by District Railway
Double royal poster
E L BAMFORD 1921

Wimbledon, with its extensive common, was advertised as countryside in Way's 1912 poster and continued to feature as such on posters until the early 1920s.

But Wimbledon Common never achieved the fame or popularity of its neighbour Richmond Park and the Underground's publicity soon concentrated on the tennis rather than on the charms of Wimbledon itself.

800 Miles in London's Country
Double crown poster
ANONYMOUS 1934

Whitsun in the Country *Panel poster*
HERRY PERRY 1934

These posters were issued to advertise three London Transport booklets of country *Strolls & Rambles*. Two books described walks that could be reached by Green Line, whose coach services radiated from central London to towns up to 39 miles into the home counties. When the Metropolitan Railway became part of London Transport in 1933, a third book was added to the series, giving details of walks that could be taken from Metropolitan Line stations among the Chiltern hills and villages.

Dogs Love the Countryside *Panel poster*
ANONYMOUS 1914

This is more than just a statutory notice informing passengers of the fare charged for taking a dog on the Underground. Its purpose is actually to promote Underground travel by letting people know that they can take their dogs for a run in the country and they are as welcome as their owners (as long as they buy the right ticket).

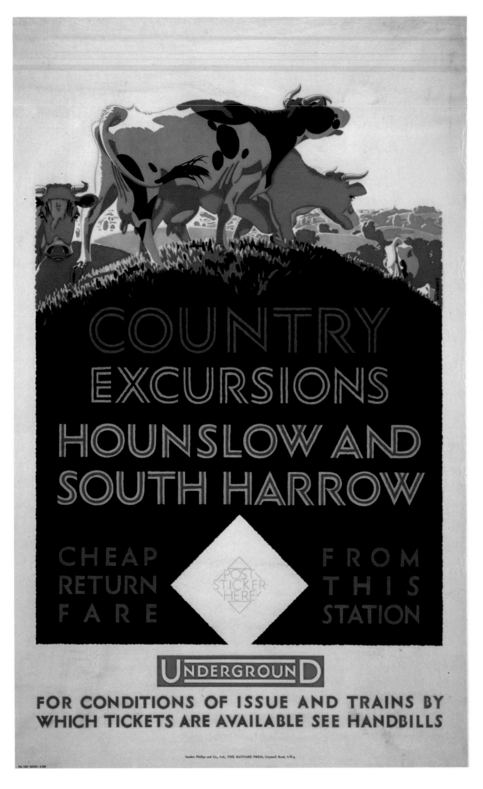

Country Excursions
Double royal poster
F C HERRICK 1926

**At London's Service
– Chalfont St Giles**
Double royal poster
WALTER E SPRADBERY 1934

When the Underground absorbed the Metropolitan Railway in 1933 to become its Metropolitan Line, it became possible to advertise a wide range of new destinations in London's country. The phrase *'At London's Service'* appeared on several sets of posters advertising places around London which could be reached by tube, bus or coach.

Spring was always a popular theme for Underground posters, and each year heralded the new season's campaign to encourage passengers to travel to the countryside by tube and bus.

Spring by Underground
Double royal poster
CHARLES PAINE 1928

Go find the Spring
Double royal poster
ALMA FAULKNER 1928

Spring in the Village
Double royal poster
EDWARD McKNIGHT KAUFFER 1936

Cheap day return tickets to the Chiltern country are issued from all Underground stations on the Metropolitan and East London Lines, daily. Sundays and Bank Holidays by all trains. Mondays to Fridays between 10 and 4. Saturdays by all trains after 10. Here (on right) are the return fares from Baker Street Station (Metropolitan Line) and from Marylebone Station (L.N.E.R.).

RICKMANSWORTH	2/3
CHORLEY WOOD	2/6
CHALFONT AND LATIMER	2/9
CHESHAM	3/3
AMERSHAM	3/-
GT. MISSENDEN	3/8
WENDOVER	4/3
STOKE MANDEVILLE	4/6

Good Spot, the Chilterns

LONDON TRANSPORT

H2N.572

Spradbery, one of the most prolific artists designing posters for the Underground, specialised in country views. The panel posters on this and the facing page, based on lino-cuts, form part of a small series. Their effectiveness is partly because of the way Spradbery incorporated the bullseye into the overall design, altering the colour to match. If there were guidelines on the use and design of the bullseye (as there are today) they seem to have been interpreted very flexibly to suit the artist's style!

Fragrance *Panel poster*
WALTER E SPRADBERY 1936

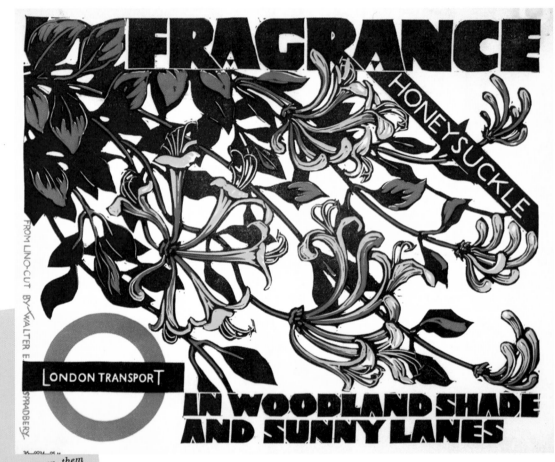

Away we go!

Here are the books for walkers: 'Country Walks', 1st, 2nd and 3rd Series. Between them they describe and map 800 miles of walks, all within 30 miles of Charing Cross. There are illustrations from seven counties, and the commentary will brighten the rainiest day. Here is surprising value. From bookstalls, newsagents, London Transport enquiry offices, certain Metropolitan Line ticket offices or London Transport, 55 Broadway, London, S.W.1. 3d. each.

Autumn Hues *Panel poster*
WALTER E SPRADBERY 1936

The Country by Underground
Double royal poster
IRENE FAWKES 1928

This simple design plays on the idea
that there is light, and in this case
countryside, at the end of the
tunnel.

Steamer Cruises
Double royal poster
ESMÉ ROBERTS 1935

Following the success of her 1934 poster design for the Port of London, Esmé Roberts was asked to produce another poster in 1935. This strong art deco design in which movement and activity are emphasised is a much more colourful version of her 1934 design.

From the earliest days the River Thames has been vital to London's development, not just as a major port, but also as a site for industry and an important means of transport. Before the advent of the horse-drawn omnibus and the first underground railways, the Thames was a major highway. But, with the arrival of the railways and parallel improvements to London's roads, this once important role quickly declined.

In addition to these industrial functions, the Thames had for many years been a place of pleasure for all Londoners. In the seventeenth century ice fairs were held on the frozen river, while in the nineteenth and early twentieth centuries punts and rowing boats could be hired, or trips taken both up and down river by steam launches.

In the early part of the twentieth century, the Underground was quick to promote those parts of the Thames which could be directly reached by its trains, or where continuation by its company's trams could connect other parts with its stations. Up-river, as far as Richmond and Kew, the Thames could be directly reached by the District Railway and these services were frequently promoted.

Connecting London United tram services between Twickenham and Hampton Court were also advertised for those wishing to travel further afield.

Closer to the centre of London, the annual boat race between Oxford and Cambridge Universities was a major sporting event popular with spectators. The Underground advertised it each year, usually on small posters displayed on the glass draught screens inside its Underground carriages. Near the City London's docks were still busy docks. Posters were issued, not as one might expect to encourage the dockers to take the Tube to work, but to encourage tourists and sightseers to take a steamer cruise from Tower Pier, to view the many commercial ships from around the world.

For a few years up to 1939 London had a small man-made beach near Tower Bridge. But this was not the sea. To spend a day or more at the seaside it was necessary to travel to the North Kent coast, Brighton or Southend. The opening of the railway from London in the mid-nineteenth century led to the villages along the Essex shore of the Thames estuary to develop rapidly in the late nineteenth century, both as dormitory towns and seaside resorts. Until the Second World War, Southend, Westcliff, Shoeburyness and Thorpe Bay were accessible by direct Underground trains. The Underground, in competition with the Great Eastern Railway's trains which ran from Liverpool Street Station to Essex coast resorts, was keen to promote its own District Railway services. This resulted in the Underground's only seaside posters.

..M. times are heavy figures	District and LMS	Through trains between Ealing and Southend-on-Sea with Branch line connections		24

	WEEKDAYS							SUNDAY	

	a.m.		Sat. excepted p.m		p.m.		Sat. excepted p.m.	Saturday only p.m.	a.m.	p.m.
..LING BROADWAY		9 32		8 36		10 46		11 9		11 9		10 28		9 59
Uxbridge	8 51		7 55		10 17		10 32		10 37		9 56		9 27
Hillingdon Swakeleys	8 53		7 57		10 19		10 34		10 39		9 58		9 29
Ickenham	8 55		7 59		10 21		10 36		10 41		10 0		9 31
Ruislip	8 58		8 2		10 24		10 39		10 44		10 3		9 34
Ruislip Manor	8 59		8 3		10 25		10 40		10 45		10 4		9 35
Eastcote	9 1		8 5											
Rayners Lane	H 9 5		H 8 9											
South Harrow	9 21		8 22											
Sudbury Hill	9 23		8 24											
Sudbury Town	9 25		8 26											
Alperton	9 27		8 28											
Park Royal Hanger Hill ...	9 29		8 30											
North Ealing	9 31		8 33											
..LING COMMON		9 35												
Hounslow West	9 19		8 25											
Hounslow Central	9 21		8 27											
Hounslow East	9 23		8 29											
Osterley	H 9 24		H 8 30											
Boston Manor	9 27		8 33											
Northfields...........	9 29		8 35											
South Ealing	9 26		8 36											
..CTON TOWN		9 38												
		9 40												
..HISWICK PARK														
Richmond	9 31		8 31											
Kew Gardens	H 9 34		H 8 34											
Gunnersbury	9 37		8 37											
..URNHAM GREEN		9 42												
..amford Brook	H 9 41		H 8 42											
..avenscourt Park	H 9 42		H 8 43											
..AMMERSMITH........		9 46												
..arons Court	C 9 45		C 8 43											
..EST KENSINGTON ..	C 9 47													
Wimbledon	9 35		8 34											
Wimbledon Park	9 37		8 36											
Southfields	9 39		8 38											
East Putney	9 42		8 40											
Putney Bridge	C 9 44		C 8 43											
Parsons Green	9 46		8 46											
Walham Green	9 43		8 47											
West Brompton	9 45		8 44											
..ARLS COURT		9 52												
..oucester Road	F 9 51		F 8 51											
..uth Kensington	F 9 53		F 8 53											
..oane Square		9 57												
..CTORIA		9 59												
..James Park		10 1												
..estminster		10 2												
..HARING CROSS		10 4												
..mple		10 5												
..ackfriars		10 7												
..ANSION HOUSE		10 9												
..nnon Street		10 10												
..onument		10 11												
..ark Lane		10 13												
..dgate East		10 16												
		10 19												
..HITECHAPEL														
..pney Green	B 10 13		B 9 11											
..le End	B 10 16		B 9 13											
..st Ham		10 33		B 9 26											
..RKING		10 45												
..genham														
..rnchurch														
..minster														
..st Horndon														
..ndon														
..seal														
..nfleet														
..igh on Sea		11 19												
..alkwell		11 23												
..stcliff on Sea		11 27												
..UTHEND ON SEA		11 32												
..uthend East		11 37												
..orpe Bay		11 41												
..OEBURYNESS		11 45												

B—Change at Barking.   C—Change at Earls Court.

Southend & Westcliff-on-Sea
Double royal poster
CHARLES SHARLAND 1908

The UNDERGROUND logotype had been introduced at the beginning of 1908, but the fact that this poster was a joint promotion with the London Tilbury & Southend Railway may explain why it does not appear here. This poster was also issued with text to promote just the LT&SR.

Southend-on-Sea
Double royal poster
VERNEY DANVERS 1924

At over a mile long and with a railway of its own, Southend's pier is probably its most famous sight. This view of the pier is taken from higher up the hill than in the 1908 poster. By 1924 the UNDERGROUND wording still appeared, while the names of the partners had changed to LM&S and L&NE Railways.

Southend-on-Sea *Double royal poster*
CHARLES PEARS 1935

In this poster of yachts Pears' skill as a marine artist comes to the fore. Through Underground services to Southend were to end four years later, on 1 October 1939, following the outbreak of the Second World War.

SOUTHEND-ON-SEA

Cheap day return fare

POST FARE STICKER HERE

From this Station

For availability and conditions of issue see leaflets obtainable at Ticket Office

DISTRICT & MIDLAND (L.T. & S.) RAILWAYS

UNDERGROUND

HALF-DAY TRIPS TO WESTCLIFF AND SOUTHEND-ON-SEA

...end Your Half-Holiday at the Seaside

TIME TABLE—DAILY, EXCEPT SATURDAYS

		P.M.	
...ALING	... dep.	1 30	On Sundays the Train starts 4 minutes earlier, and Trains return from Southend at 6.25 and 7.40 (and 10.0 p.m. from 28th June to 6th Sept. inclusive, to Ealing and Putney and Wimbledon lines only).
...CTON TOWN...	... "	1 33	
...URNHAM GREEN	... "	1 37	
...AMMERSMITH	... "	1 40	
...ARL'S COURT...	... "	1 44	
...ICTORIA	... "	1 49	
...ESTCLIFF	... arr.	3 2	
...OUTHEND-ON-SEA	... arr.	3 6	

Return Trains leave Southend on Week-days at 6.30, 7.10, 8.8, 9.10, 10.5 (from 27th June to 5th September inclusive) and 10.30* p.m.

Return Fares range from 2/11 from Ealing, to 2/6 from Temple, 3rd Class.

CONVENIENT CONNECTING TRAINS

From Uxbridge, South Harrow, Hounslow, Richmond, Wimbledon and Putney Branches, at corresponding Fares. See Handbills giving Fares.

* There is no connection by this train to Stations from Rayners Lane to Uxbridge, inclusive.

Half-day trips to Westcliff and Southend-on-Sea *Leaflet*
ANONYMOUS June 1914

The introduction, on 1 June 1910, of a through District service from Ealing saw a dramatic increase in the amount of the Underground's publicity for holidays in Southend. Few opportunities were lost to generate extra traffic, with the Underground even encouraging half-day trips to the coast.

The Underground and the 'Call to the East Coast' *Leaflet*
ANONYMOUS 1914

New opportunities were keenly promoted but this one was to prove short lived. The outbreak of the First World War prevented a similar arrangement from running in the following years.

THE **UNDERGROUND** AND THE "CALL TO THE EAST COAST"

NEW ARRANGEMENTS BETWEEN THE DISTRICT & MIDLAND (L.T.S.) RAILWAYS & "BELLE" STEAMERS

TIME AND TROUBLE SAVED

Commencing 30th May, 1914, convenient Trains will be run on District Railway to Barking, connecting with the "Belle" Boat Trains via Tilbury Pier.

Passengers will be able to obtain at District Railway Stations Cheap 3rd Class Return Tickets to Tilbury Pier, and to the holders of such tickets on presentation at the Booking Office at Tilbury, Reduced Rate Saloon Tickets will be issued by the "Belle" Steamers, so that such passengers can travel expeditiously from the Western and Central portions of London by the "Belle" Steamers for the East Coast Resorts at no increase in the Fares, as against joining the Boat at London Bridge.

FOR PARTICULARS OF TIMES OF TRAINS AND FARES SEE OTHER SIDE

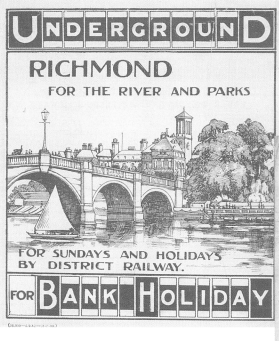

Richmond for the River and Parks
Timetable leaflet
ANONYMOUS 1908

Richmond for the River and Parks
Poster
ANONYMOUS 1908

Both the illustrated cover to the timetable, containing details of trains to Richmond, and the poster use the new UNDERGROUND logo, which was introduced following the London Passenger Traffic Conference on 29 February 1908. They are a good example of a co-ordinated campaign in which posters and leaflets complement each other. The two views of the sailing boat approaching Richmond Bridge are the same, except that the one on the poster has been printed by lithography while that on the leaflet is a much cruder and cheaper wood cut. The use of block lettering on the bottom of the leaflet mirroring the lettering at the top is unusual on Underground publicity.

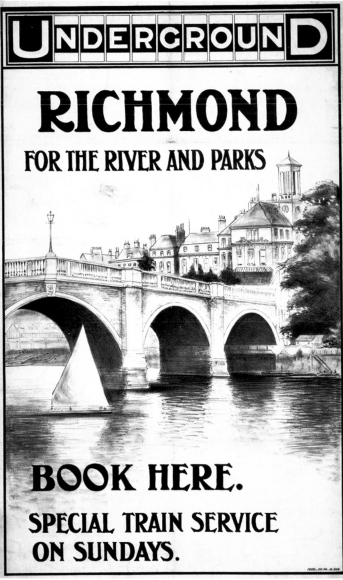

Despite the growth of London, the Thames as it approaches Westminster still retains some of its earlier and more rural charms and in this poster of 1912 not a building can be seen. Although it was possible to reach Twickenham from central London directly by the London & South Western Railway, this poster recommends the Underground route to Richmond (also an L & S W R station).

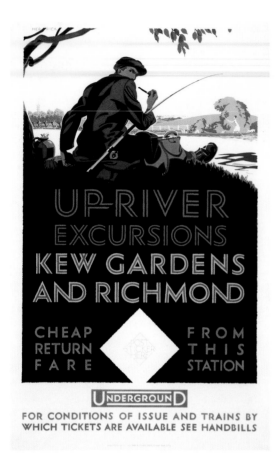

Up-river Excursions
Double royal poster
F C HERRICK 1925

Herrick, one of England's leading poster designers, produced many memorable designs for the Underground. The phrase 'up-river' was used on many Underground posters to promote the delights of Kew, Richmond and Twickenham. Kew Gardens, linked here with Richmond, was the subject for many posters, appearing at least once a year. Once again the use of Johnston typeface has been mixed with another sympathetic face, probably by Herrick or his assistant.

Up-river Excursions
Double royal poster
KATE BURRELL 1927

This poster, also for Kew and Richmond, is typical of Kate Burrell's posters in which a small vignette sits above the text and the whole is framed by a decorative border. Just visible in the background between the trees is the unmistakable landmark of the Pagoda at Kew.

Regatta-time's pleasant
Double royal poster
JEAN DUPAS 1933

In 1933, with the formation of the London Passenger Transport Board, a new logo was introduced. Designed by C W Bacon, the winged symbol only lasted a short while and was soon replaced by the familiar, and slightly re-proportioned, bullseye.

"Regatta-time's pleasant
Thrice pleasant in laughing July."

Richmond Station for the River

The River 'Derby'
Double royal poster
ARTHUR WATTS 1926

This double royal size poster is an exception to the practice of using small panels to promote the Boat Race and is a fine example of the use of Johnston lettering.

Boat Race
Panel poster
A E MARTY 1933

In 1933 Marty designed a set of 13 panel posters for the Underground, all for sporting or special events. With a minimal use of flat colour and sparing use of detail, Marty created striking and simple designs. His work as a fashion illustrator can be clearly seen in his elegantly drawn woman and child.

Head of the River Race
Panel poster
DAVIES 1939

This montage by Davies contrasts strongly with other posters of the Boat Race. Here, there is no sign of a spectator – nor even a boat! In addition to the Underground stations listed, this and the previous year's posters for the Head of the River Race, rather surprisingly, also included stations of the rival Southern Railway.

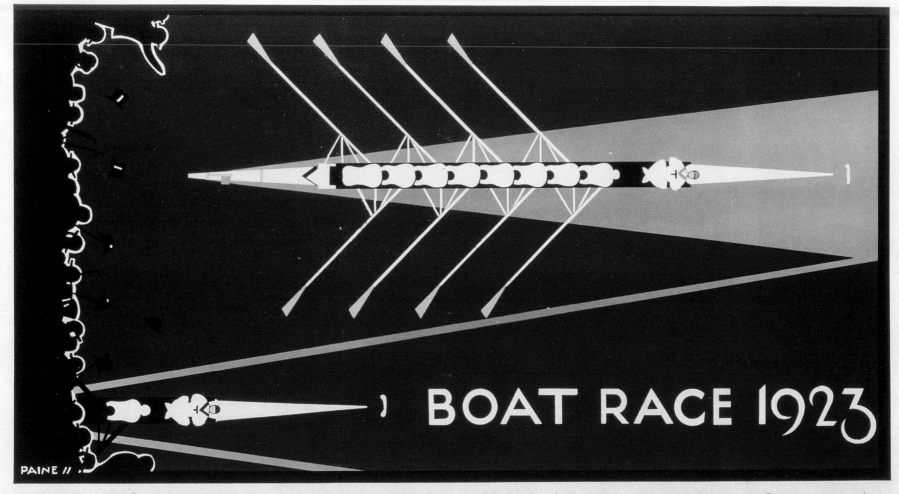

Boat Race 1923 *Panel poster*
CHARLES PAINE 1923

The Boat Race has always featured among London's most important sporting occasions. In the days before television, huge crowds would attend and the Underground would lay on additional trains to cope with the expected influx. In the 1920s and 1930s the annual Boat Race posters would take the form of small panels for display inside the Underground carriages, either in the advertising spaces or on the glass draught screens alongside the sliding doors.

Boat Race *Panel poster*
KATE BURRELL 1924

Although Kate Burrell designed 15 posters for the Underground between 1924 and 1934, nothing is known of this talented designer. Many of the Boat Race posters include a view of the bridges it passes, no doubt because they offered among the best views.

The Boat Race Centenary
Panel poster
R T COOPER 1929

Cooper specialised in portraying historic events; this time recreating a view of the first ever university boat race.

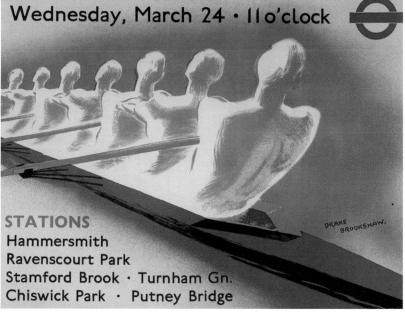

Saturday March 31st *Panel poster*
P DRAKE BROOKSHAW 1928

The Boat Race's fame made it not even necessary to spell out what this poster was advertising. The image of two teams rowing and the date of the competition was sufficient. The names of the stations ensured that the spectator got the message to travel there by Underground.

Wednesday March 24
Panel poster
P DRAKE BROOKSHAW 1937

This is Brookshaw's second poster for the Boat Race. Surprisingly, he did not receive another commission from London Transport until 1958, a gap of over 20 years.

**Cheap Fares for
School & Pleasure Parties**
Double royal poster
KATE BURRELL 1928

From its earliest days the Underground had trouble in meeting its financial targets and needed to find ways to increase its income. As a private company it was undesirable to run at a loss and therefore needed to develop new markets. Fortunately there was spare capacity on its trains at weekends, public holidays and either side of the morning and early evening rush hours.

To encourage travel at these off-peak times the Underground started to produce posters advertising some of the many delights to be found in and around London which were accessible by the Underground. Most of this publicity was aimed at the individual or family, but the Underground also aimed some at groups.

School and Sunday School parties were among the first groups to be targeted. Much of the early publicity was for the District Railway for the simple reason that while the early tube railways were still developing and their short lines limited mainly to urban London, the District (part of the Underground Group from 1902), was a fully fledged railway reaching to Hounslow and Uxbridge, which was far beyond the confines of London's urban centre.

These group outings were never a major market for the Underground. Nevertheless, half a million pleasure party tickets were sold annually, and they were considered important enough to need their own publicity in the form of posters and leaflets. Much of this publicity showed illustrations of children enjoying themselves in the open air, either the countryside or one of London's many parks. The purpose of most of these leaflets was to promote not just tube travel to groups, but bus and coach travel as well. Nor were they aimed at groups travelling just to London's parks and countryside but equally to the city's many tourist sights.

The Underground described almost every type of pleasure trip as an *outing* and often did not make it clear in its publicity if groups or individuals were being targeted. Although for many years the Underground produced an annual colourful poster and accompanying booklet aimed at the school and group market, it also tried to encourage individuals and families to enjoy a special outing by tube or bus. In the 1920s and 1930s this resulted in an attractive series of colourful leaflets encouraging Londoners to take a pleasure trip at Easter, Whitsun and August Bank Holiday. These leaflets are among some of the most attractive the Underground ever produced.

The Open Gate *Double royal poster*
F C Herrick 1925

School and Pleasure Parties *Booklet*
F C Herrick 1925

This booklet, which was also reissued in 1926, was a redrawn version of the poster. The portrayal of the Underground as London's gateway to the countryside was often found on the Underground's publicity leaflets and posters. The design was not just simplified to adapt it to the smaller scale of the booklet. The billowing smoke and the gate with the UNDERGROUND logo on it were also reversed.

School & Pleasure Parties
Double royal poster
Kate Burrell 1927

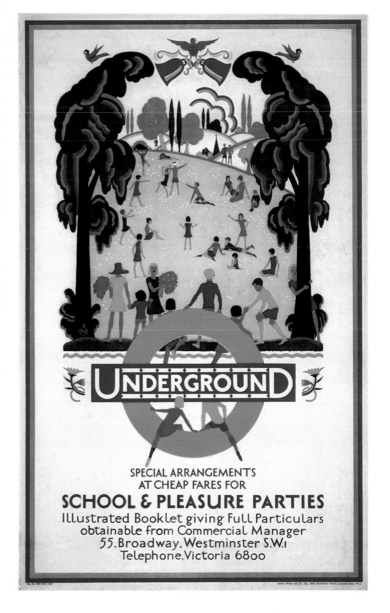

In Search of Happiness *Leaflet*
MABEL LUCIE ATTWELL 1914

The illustration on this leaflet giving
details of school outings was also
used on a poster, as were most of the
designs promoting school outings.
This is one of the earliest examples
of a co-ordinated campaign of
poster and leaflet for school trips.

**You Can Reach the Heart of the
Country** *Booklet*
Probably HOLDSWORTH 1923

This attractive booklet, believed to
be by Holdsworth, has colour
illustrations throughout. There is a
page for each letter of the alphabet
with an appropriate verse. On the
opposite pages are details of fares.

**Sunday School and
Pleasure Outing Resorts Served by
District Rly** *Leaflet*
ANONYMOUS 1915

Surprisingly, the Underground
Group issued two leaflets for School
and Pleasure Outings in 1915,
which seems an unnecessary luxury
during wartime. Ironically, inside
the leaflet is the message, *As a result
of the War all special cheap fares for
Pleasure Parties have necessarily been
cancelled by all Railway Companies*; a
slight contradiction to the statement
on the front cover saying 'At Fares
which are always Cheap'!

Pleasure Outings on the District Railway *Booklet*
HOLDSWORTH 1922

Occasionally the Underground would go to the expense of producing a colour booklet advertising a particular service. Usually the use of colour was limited to the front and, occasionally, also to the back cover where it would be seen. Holdsworth's stylised illustrations represent children's wooden toys of the period. Note also, the hand drawn lettering.

Most of the Underground's publicity material can be dated from the print code to be found at the bottom left or right side (on the back if it is a leaflet or booklet). On this booklet the print code gives a date of 1915, yet the date inside is May 1922. It is possible that the cover was designed in 1915 but not used then, perhaps because of the war. Equally, the cover might have actually been printed but stored, when the prospect of the war as a lengthy stalemate became more apparent.

Perhaps it was because there was doubt in people's minds that the Underground did actually reach out to the country that the Underground believed there was a need to state that its trains reached the 'real country'. A more realistic representation of the country might also have helped.

The Underground allowed a large amount of artistic licence in its publicity, but the last steam hauled passenger trains ran on the District Railway in 1912.

In the 1920s a remarkable transformation came over the small leaflets listing train, bus and tram times for holiday travel. In the immediate years following the end of the First World War they were printed in sepia or black and white, usually with a poor quality photograph on the cover. By 1922 Frank Pick must have decided it was time to bring these leaflets into line with the design qualities of the posters. They were printed in two or three colours and designed by the best commercial designers of the period. Often the image appeared on both the leaflet and on a sticker which would be used to brighten up an otherwise colourless typographic poster. However, in the mid-1930s photographs began to be used again on some of the leaflets, resulting in much less eye-catching covers.

Bank Holiday Excursions, August 1920 *Leaflet*
HAROLD STABLER 1920

Holiday Outings *Leaflet*
MRS G BARRACLOUGH 1922

Your Whitsun Holiday *Leaflet*
ANONYMOUS 1924

Your Chance to Change from Grey to Green *Double royal poster*
VERA WILLOUGHBY 1934

Bank Holiday Where to Go August *Leaflet*
HORACE TAYLOR 1924

Easter Holiday How to Spend It *Leaflet*
ANONYMOUS 1925

Bank Holiday Where to Go *Leaflet*
DORA M BATTY 1926

BY TRAIN TRAM
AND MOTOR BUS

EASTER
1927

PROGRAMME OF
EXCURSIONS
TRAIN TRAM
AND OMNIBUS

AUGUST
BANK HOLIDAY
PROGRAMME
1927

LONDON'S UNDERGROUND

WHITSUN
PROGRAMME
1928

LONDON'S UNDERGROUND

August Bank Holiday
Panel poster
RICHARD BECK
1935

August Bank Holiday
Double royal poster
EDWARD MCKNIGHT
KAUFFER 1937

WHITSUNTIDE

PROGRAMME OF
EXCURSIONS
BY TRAIN –
BUS – TRAM

EASTER 1930

BY
LONDON'S
UNDERGROUND

LONDON &
LONDON'S
COUNTRY
BY
LONDON'S UNDERGROUND
SUMMER
1930

EASTER
IN THE COUNTRY

BY
LONDON'S
UNDERGROUND

**Come Out of Your Shell,
Easter** *Leaflet*
CHARLES PAINE 1927

Whitsuntide 1927
Leaflet
ANONYMOUS 1927

**August Bank Holiday
Programme 1927** *Leaflet*
BERNARD KEARLY 1927

**Whitsun Programme
1928** *Leaflet*
CHARLES SHEPHERD 1928

Whitsuntide 1929
Leaflet
EDWARD MCKNIGHT
KAUFFER 1929

Easter 1930 *Leaflet*
ANONYMOUS 1930

Summer 1930 *Leaflet*
KATE BURRELL 1930

Easter in the Country
Leaflet
TOM GENTLEMAN 1932

Pleasure Outings
Double royal poster
HERRY PERRY 1935

Herry Perry was one of the more prolific women artists designing posters for the Underground, often in a humorous or light-hearted style.

Cheap Fares
Double royal poster/leaflet
FREDA LINGSTROM 1929

The girl dancing among the flowers was substantially redrawn for the booklet promoted in the poster. To fit the booklet's smaller size and narrower format the number of flowers was reduced and the girl's arm raised further above her head.

Pleasure Parties & School Outings
Leaflet
ARNRID JOHNSTON 1934

Johnston's booklet was almost exactly the same proportion as the poster which advertised it. There was, therefore, no need to redraw the image for the poster.

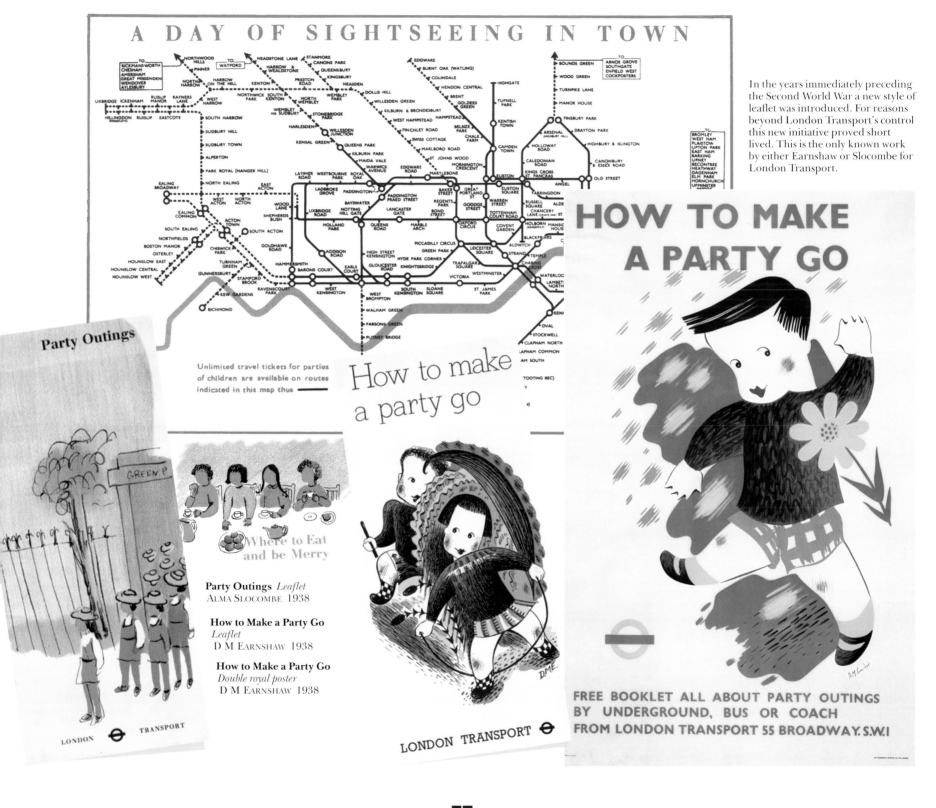

A DAY OF SIGHTSEEING IN TOWN

Unlimited travel tickets for parties of children are available on routes indicated in this map thus ——

How to make a party go

In the years immediately preceding the Second World War a new style of leaflet was introduced. For reasons beyond London Transport's control this new initiative proved short lived. This is the only known work by either Earnshaw or Slocombe for London Transport.

Party Outings

Where to Eat and be Merry

Party Outings *Leaflet*
ALMA SLOCOMBE 1938

How to Make a Party Go
Leaflet
D M EARNSHAW 1938

How to Make a Party Go
Double royal poster
D M EARNSHAW 1938

LONDON TRANSPORT

HOW TO MAKE A PARTY GO

FREE BOOKLET ALL ABOUT PARTY OUTINGS
BY UNDERGROUND, BUS OR COACH
FROM LONDON TRANSPORT 55 BROADWAY. S.W.1

BIBLIOGRAPHY

Christian Barman, **The Man Who Built London Transport**,
David & Charles, 1979

Mark Haworth Booth, **E McKnight Kauffer**,
Gordon Fraser, 1979

David Ruddom *and* Gerrard Roots, **Getting There by Road,
Rail and Air in Barnet**, *London Borough of Barnet*, 1983

Ken Garland, **Mr Beck's Underground Map**,
Capital Transport, 1994

Oliver Green, **Underground Art**, *Studio Vista*, 1990

David Lawrence, **Bar & Circle**, *Capital Transport*, 1998

Jonathan Riddell *and* William Sterne,
By Underground to Kew, *Studio Vista*, 1994

Jonathan Riddell *and* Peter Denton,
By Underground to The Zoo, *Studio Vista*, 1995

Ben Weinreb *and* Christopher Hibbert,
The London Encyclopaedia, *MacMillan*, 1983

Michael Levy, **London Transport Posters**,
Phaidon/London Transport, 1976